"This book provides a practical, common-sense guide to the main stumbling blocks facing business leaders and how to deal with them."

—John Quelch, dean of China Europe International
Business School (CEIBS), Shanghai and former
associate dean, Harvard Business School

"This book is a great gift to leaders facing the eight barriers because it underscores how critical it is to engage employees across the entire organization. Dumb things, goodbye!"

—Frances Hesselbein, president and CEO of Frances Hesselbein
Leadership Institute, former CEO of Girl Scouts of
the USA, and author, *My Life in Leadership*

"A helpful reminder on how lack of oversight on even commonplace issues can interfere with an enterprise's productivity and success, this work will appeal to managers and leaders alike."

—*Publishers Weekly*

D1533763

HOW EXCELLENT COMPANIES AVOID DUMB THINGS

HOW EXCELLENT COMPANIES AVOID DUMB THINGS

BREAKING THE 8 HIDDEN BARRIERS THAT PLAGUE EVEN THE BEST BUSINESSES

NEIL SMITH
WITH PATRICIA O'CONNELL

palgrave
macmillan

HOW EXCELLENT COMPANIES AVOID DUMB THINGS
Copyright © NTS, LLC, 2012.

First published in hardcover in 2012 by PALGRAVE MACMILLAN® in the
US—a division of St. Martin's Press LLC, 175 Fifth Avenue, New York,
NY 10010.

Where this book is distributed in the UK, Europe and the rest of the world,
this is by Palgrave Macmillan, a division of Macmillan Publishers Limited,
registered in England, company number 785998, of Houndmills,
Basingstoke, Hampshire RG21 6XS.

Palgrave Macmillan is the global academic imprint of the above companies
and has companies and representatives throughout the world.

Palgrave® and Macmillan® are registered trademarks in the United States,
the United Kingdom, Europe and other countries.

ISBN 978–1–137–27840–1

Library of Congress Cataloging-in-Publication Data

Smith, Neil.
    How excellent companies avoid dumb things : breaking the 8 hidden barriers
that plague even the best businesses / Neil Smith with Patricia O'Connell.
        p. cm.
    1. Organizational effectiveness. 2. Decision making. 3. Psychology, Industrial.
    4. Management. 5. Success in business. I. O'Connell, Patricia. II. Title.

HD58.9.S643 2012
658.4—dc23   2011049321

A catalogue record of the book is available from the British Library.

Design by Newgen Knowledge Works (P) Ltd., Chennai, India

First PALGRAVE MACMILLAN paperback edition: September 2013

10 9 8 7 6 5 4 3 2 1

Printed in the United States of America.

To my beautiful wife, Gina—the person who helps me avoid dumb things—for her love, patience, and understanding. She is my rock. Without her belief and encouragement, it is hard to imagine where my life would have led. And to my daughters Brianna, Caroline, and Charlotte and to my son, Alex, who light up our lives and are an inspiration to us with their enthusiasm, good grace, and humor. I have discovered the real meaning of life. Thank you, and love to each of you.

CONTENTS

AUTHOR'S NOTE

I WOULD LIKE TO THANK THOSE GREAT LEADERS WHO gave liberally of their time to add their own experiences to make this book better. I have been very fortunate that many of my former clients have turned into good friends. It never ceases to amaze me how these busy people share freely the one thing they don't have much of—their time. Although the book is filled with real-world examples of opportunity, some of the names, data, company examples, and even industries have been disguised to protect the confidentiality of the companies and the identities of the individuals involved.

This book would never have been written without the leadership shown by Patricia O'Connell. From the time I first met Patricia in her *Businessweek* days, we were kindred spirits. She identified immediately with the story I wanted to tell, and she saw the potential in this book. Through the long hours, the tight deadlines, and the healthy debate, she took my thoughts and made them clearer and took my words and made them sparkle. All the things you like about the book and the way it is written are thanks to her; if a point is unclear, then I probably sneaked it in against her better judgment.

The evening I had cocktails under the fading Southern California sun with Dr. Richard Levak and his wonderful wife, Linda, would prove fortuitous. Richard, one of the leading experts in human behavior, was fresh from his latest appearance on *Larry King Live* and listened with great interest to what I do. As I explained to him my observations about hidden barriers, he explained to me why so many of them were predictable from a human behavior point of view. I am honored that he contributed some of his keen intellect and understanding to this book.

About 15 years ago I had the good fortune to meet Gene Ludwig, then comptroller of the currency in the United States and now the chief executive of Promontory. Anyone who meets Gene instantly recognizes his wisdom and his insights. Just as his initiatives transformed (in a measureable way) the banking system in the 1990s, his insight transformed my own efforts to perfect a process. In the late 1990s, Gene correctly reasoned that the quest to improve performance should not be confined to companies that were struggling. Indeed, some of the world's best companies were looking for a fast and painless way to become less complex and more profitable. This insight transformed the way I do business, and he was responsible for finding my previous firm its first true industry leader as a client. Now I am even more fortunate than I was then. For the last three years, I have been proud to call Gene my partner.

Alfred Moses keeps me on track and helps me maintain a sense of perspective. An advisor to three presidents, his words of wisdom have been appreciated by many people far more important than I am, which makes me all the more grateful that he takes an active interest in the clients we are serving and how we serve them.

The success of my work with my clients cannot really be attributed to me but rather to the senior colleagues I worked with on each of those assignments. I first met Jan Nicolson when she was head of human resources at a former client. My work would not be possible without her keen intuition and instincts. Dr. Fred Weling has worked with me on a number of projects. The same process, with small variations, has been used by no fewer than five companies that have employed me over the years. The process we now use combines the best of these experiences, and Fred is the keeper of it. Melanie Lindsay has much experience working on both sides of the Atlantic and brings an international flavor to what we do. Her wisdom and knowledge guide much of our thinking. George Swetlitz is probably one of the most experienced practitioners of the art of improvement. Like me, he has spent more than 20 years working on this process or its forerunners. We first worked together, with a very primitive version of the process described in this book, in Indonesia in the 1980s. Gina Macdonald leads by example. Her quiet but firm guidance is well respected by everyone she works with. I would also like to thank Laura Katona for all the administrative coordination that goes into writing a book and Kathy Villella, who is responsible for the creativity in compiling the charts that I use.

From my very first discussion with Laurie Harting at Palgrave Macmillan, she added value to the book. It was clear that she immediately understood the hidden barriers, and her passion and focus have guided me and this book every step along the way. I cannot imagine working with another editor after working with Laurie. She has to be the best at what she does. My thanks go to her and her colleagues, who truly made this book possible.

Neil Smith
Chief Executive Officer
Promontory Growth and Innovation
New York

www.neilsmithinsights.com

INTRODUCTION: HIDDEN GOLD

MOST MANAGEMENT BOOKS BEGIN WITH A THEORY and then look for empirical evidence and observations to support that theory. This one is different. I began with a startling observation, made over the last 20 years, and I wanted to figure out why I kept on seeing the same phenomenon over and over. *Every* company has a staggeringly huge opportunity to do what it does even better. I don't think it's possible that your company can improve its performance. I *know* your company can do so. Dozens of companies I have worked with over the last 20 years prove this point.

How do I know your company is like all the others? Because there are two things that every single company has: hidden barriers that prevent great ideas from surfacing . . . and employees with great ideas for how the company can do things differently.

One of my clients was a medical services company that worked on behalf of life insurance companies. Insurance companies need to know about the health of the person being insured before they write a policy, so they will send a nurse to perform a physical examination at the home of the person who wants to be insured. The exam includes listening to the heart, checking the blood pressure, and taking a blood sample.

Rightly or wrongly, insurance companies do not want to insure people who have been exposed to the HIV virus, so that is one of the things the blood sample will be tested for. Insurance companies have been known to test 80-year-olds for the virus.

Once a blood sample is turned in to the lab, the average test costs $5 to carry out. My client was performing more than two million of these blood tests a year. The bill for HIV testing was running at more than $10 million annually.

One of the workers in the lab had an idea. "Why," he thought, "don't we combine the blood samples from 20 individuals and run just one test on the mixed sample? If it is negative, we know all 20 blood samples are negative. If it is positive, we will have to test each of the 20 samples once more individually to find which one is infected."

It was a brilliant idea. People with AIDS or who are HIV positive do not usually apply for life insurance policies. As a result, the vast majority of samples were uninfected, and the amount of retesting proved to be negligible. The number of AIDS-related tests performed was reduced by about 90 percent. Management was thrilled at the huge savings this idea produced.

But what is startling about this idea is not its simplicity or its impact. It is how close it came to never being implemented. You see, the lab worker had first thought of this idea seven years earlier but had not been able to implement it. And the idea was not the only one of its kind in the company. Hundreds of ideas were surfaced to make the company more efficient.

With this large number of ideas for improving the performance of the company, you may assume with some justification that the organization was poorly managed. But the management team was strong, engaged, and close to the business. What management was witnessing was a phenomenon I have seen in every company with which I have worked over the last 20 years. And many of those companies have been the best at what they do. The company and its employees were hitting hidden barriers. My experience has shown that when a company asks its employees what it can do better—and, most importantly, removes the barriers to change—the results are staggering.

My experience at this company and many others has convinced me that every company, no matter the sector or the size, no matter whether it is an industry leader or an industry laggard, is sitting on a goldmine of untapped ideas. The question is how to mine the gold by identifying and removing hidden barriers. That is what this book is about.

It is time to reveal and to break the barriers, and let those brilliant employee ideas bubble up to the surface. They won't all be good—but enough of them will be to make a difference. How big a difference? On average, companies have seen literally thousands of ideas emerge, resulting in a profit boost of a massive 25 percent. But just as important, they have become less complex and easier for customers to do business with. As one chief executive put it, "Both our employees and our customers love our new way of doing business."

And imagine how those extra profits can be used. At a recent breakfast hosted by the head of a Fortune 250 company and attended by senior management of other companies, the hosting CEO, Dan, asked, "How many of you think your company had invested sufficiently over the last five years?" Not a single hand was raised. At a time of inadequate investment, these freed-up funds can go even further to build stronger companies.

You are probably thinking that I have worked only with distressed companies, where there was nowhere to go but up, and that I helped companies pick the low-hanging fruit and solve the obvious problems. Certainly there cannot be untapped opportunity at a well-managed company like yours. Why would excellent companies do "dumb" things? How could your leadership team be responsible for leaving money on the table?

But the opportunity is found in even the best-managed, most successful companies that have great leaders. More than half of the companies I have worked with are considered to be in the top three in their industry. How can even the best management teams have overlooked so much opportunity? This book answers that question...and provides a road map for finding the hidden treasure in your company.

Just over 20 years ago, I finished my stint as a consultant with one of the top global consulting companies. During my 5 years there, I had 19 assignments alongside some extremely smart people, and I worked with the CEOs of some of the world's most famous companies. Initially the idea of helping great companies get even better had been very exciting.

But I wasn't sure I was really doing that. Once we gave the company our recommendations, I was never sure whether any change was implemented because it was not our job to oversee implementation. In fact, at most companies, I don't think it was anyone's job.

While I was not able to follow up with those companies formally—after all, I was off to the next assignment—I could follow them in the news and through the friends I had made while working with them. The recommendations were not being implemented. I was convinced that there was a need for a different approach to effecting change in companies. It had to be internally driven and owned, there had to be accountability, and the results had to be measureable. I will discuss this principle in chapter 9.

Together, my partner, my co-writer, and I have had the good fortune to meet almost 500 CEOs of Fortune 1000 companies over the past few years. In my view, great leaders are men and women with vision—individuals who know exactly the direction an organization should strive toward and who have the skills to take it there. They are positive and passionate, decisive and direct. They are genuinely interested in those around them and have the ability to motivate and inspire. They have an impeccable sense of timing. They pick and choose the right battles to fight. Great leaders are associated with growth and success.

But the organizations they lead, which often are large and complex, also strive for simplicity and efficiency. Great leaders want to become as efficient as possible in a way that is fast, does not distract from the prime focus of the business, produces very significant results, and has the complete buy-in of the organization.

So what is stopping these leaders? A series of natural barriers exists in every organization simply because of the way all companies are organized and do business. We call those *structural barriers*. Other barriers exist because of human nature. Those are the *behavioral barriers*. All of the barriers, individually and collectively, prevent employees from taking actions that are in the best interests of the company. In short, the barriers are the reason a company does dumb things, not the employees themselves.

Think about your own company and your own experiences there. Are there ten things the company could do better? My guess is you could easily come up with ten on your own. So why haven't they been done? It is the hidden barriers at work.

Armed with these insights, I have identified the eight hidden barriers that cause excellent companies to do dumb things; this book will reveal them, one by one. Understanding the barriers is only the first step in breaking them down. I also outline twelve principles for change, explain how important psychology is in making change happen, and describe a structured process that helps companies remove these barriers. These principles and the process they govern have helped achieve enormous results by generating thousands of ideas to simplify the way companies work and improve their profits. Finally I describe the staggering results that you should expect to achieve in your company. Done the right way, such a process can radically simplify the way your company works and improve profitability by 25 percent or more.

THE EIGHT BARRIERS

You will see that the leading letter in each of the eight barriers forms an acronym: "A Promise." This makes the barriers easy to remember and identify.

Avoiding Controversy
Poor Use of Time
Reluctance to Change
Organizational Silos
Management Blockers
Incorrect Information and Bad Assumptions
Size Matters
Existing Processes

For each of the eight barriers, I give several examples of how the barrier manifested itself in different companies, most of which my colleagues or I have worked with. Some you will find amusing, others insightful. In some cases you will wonder how a company can act in the way it does. In all cases it is the barriers at work—and I have found every one of them, to a greater or lesser extent, present in every company I have worked with. And they show up at every level.

I also dive into each barrier in more detail, giving some insight into why it exists and what it took to break it in each of the examples I describe. And most of the ideas for change are not mine; they come from the employees all across the organization. Three of the eight barriers are behavioral, and a fourth includes an element that is behavioral. For each of those behavioral barriers, Dr. Richard Levak has written a short essay about why normal human behavior predicts the existence of that barrier. Richard is one of the leading human behavior experts in the United States. His expertise is in great demand from reality TV programs, as they select interesting (and sometimes deliberately conflicting) personalities for their shows.

Throughout the book, I often refer to "a good change process." I introduce you to one such process (the PGI Promise®) that combines the best elements from other processes I have used over the years and that have worked dozens of times before. But it is by no means the only change process that works. PGI refers to my company, Promontory Growth and Innovation. Why is the word *promise* used? Not only is it the barrier acronym, but my belief in the power of our change process is so great that whenever I work with a company, I make this promise: we guarantee to dramatically and quickly increase the simplicity and profit of your company...or we work for free. By "my clients," I mean those companies whose projects I have led, even though I may have been working for a company when doing it.

One of the important elements to breaking down the barriers is culture change—and that is mentioned frequently in the book. That the process must be about culture change is one of the principles—and as you would expect, it is also one of the results. Culture is about the way companies do things. It is about what is expected, what is tolerated, what is encouraged, and what is supported. Culture change is important because it is a key ingredient in breaking down the behavioral barriers. It is also key to making sure the barriers remain broken down. I will describe the type of culture change that is important and how it can be achieved.

THE 12 PRINCIPLES FOR BREAKING BARRIERS

1. The process is personally led by the CEO and supported by senior management.
2. The entire organization is engaged—not merely involved—in the change process.
3. The process is guided by a sprinkling of superstars from within the organization who are willing to challenge the status quo.
4. There are no upfront targets for the company as a whole or for individual groups within it.
5. The ideas are owned by the people responsible for implementing them.
6. The ideas are easy to put into the process but hard to remove.
7. The consideration of ideas is based on facts and analysis, not opinion.
8. Consensus is built so that everyone who will be affected by a change must agree with it before it is made. (This is the real secret to removing barriers.)
9. There is a focus on increasing revenue, not only on reducing expenses.
10. The process of breaking down the barriers will not disrupt normal business.
11. Anything less than 100 percent implementation is not acceptable.
12. The change process is about culture change; this is not simply a matter of completing a project.

This book is the result of a 20-year journey to help companies unearth the enormous opportunity that exists in each of them. My hope is that it will provide insight into the huge opportunity, why that opportunity exists, the correct way to find it, and how to get the most benefit from it. I hope this book will inspire you to find the "hidden gold."

CHAPTER 1

BARRIER 1: AVOIDING CONTROVERSY

MY COLLEGE ROOMMATE WAS VERY EXCITED WHEN he called to tell me that he had been made regional manager of the pharmaceutical distributor he worked for. He had worked hard and fully deserved his promotion, which probably was overdue. "Now I can finally make some decisions to get this place moving," he said. His enthusiasm was centered on something we all believe to be true: managers make decisions and direct others. But in every company I have worked with, this truism turns out to be not quite so true. In every company, large, controversial issues are left unresolved because decisions have not been made. And these unresolved issues exist at every level of management in even the best companies.

This happens because managers often *deliberately* avoid making controversial decisions. One of the key skills of being a strong manager is knowing which battles to fight and which to ignore. The best managers have a knack for getting this just right. They have impeccable timing. They know exactly when to make a decision. They also know that it is sometimes easier and even wiser in the short run to leave things the way they are rather than to make a decision that, although obviously the right thing to do, may have other consequences. But leaders are expected to deal with and resolve controversial issues. When they do not, however good the reason, they can cause confusion, frustration, and misunderstanding as well as inefficiency.

Avoiding controversy is one of the most significant behavioral barriers, and in its wake important issues remain unresolved, usually leaving huge opportunities for change.

There are many reasons people avoid controversy and try to keep the peace, but as Neville Chamberlain learned in the years before World War II, "peace in our time" carries a high price indeed. In this chapter, I demonstrate why managers avoid controversy and what can happen when they do. And I show how a good change process can provide the air cover to tackle controversial decisions.

As you will see with all the eight barriers we write about, recognizing when a barrier exists is the first step toward breaking it. The goal of a good change process is to help companies see how each of the eight barriers manifests itself in their organizations and how they can break them down. In the case of the Avoiding Controversy barrier, it is usually very clear to the organization that decisions are not being made, but it is unclear why a manager is avoiding making them. There is usually a sound reason, but the reason is often invisible. A good change process will force controversial issues to be addressed and decisions to be made by spotlighting the issues and making avoiding a decision very difficult.

HOW AVOIDING CONTROVERSY FORCES COMPANIES TO DO DUMB THINGS

A chief executive officer of a Midwest industrial company had been living for four years with the pet project of his chief operating officer—an expansion into the "middle market," a customer base that was smaller in size than the company's traditional customer base. The venture was still considered a start-up and had yet to make a profit. The argument, year after unprofitable year, was "Oh, give us another year and we'll make money next year." The project had been approved at a time when the economy was growing quickly and it was hard for industrial companies that already served the market to keep up with demand. After two years of solid investment, it should have generated healthy profits in the third year.

This start-up was launched with much fanfare within the company. A lot of effort and money were invested in it, and its progress was featured prominently on the company's intranet—until it became apparent that the expansion wasn't going well.

The CEO was in a tough spot. The COO had been at the company much longer than he had, and many people who had thought the COO deserved the top job were disappointed when an outsider was brought in. The CEO knew that he could justify keeping this project going for only so long before the board and shareholders would ask questions, but he also knew that killing the COO's pet project would harm the COO's reputation and a relationship that was important to him.

The CEO didn't feel comfortable turning to the COO and just saying, "We need to close this down." So the expansion continued...and continued to lose money.

Why should a CEO feel uncomfortable telling a direct report, "Well, we gave it a shot, but it's just not working"? This is business, after all, and everyone is a professional. The industrial company was publicly traded, so the CEO had an obligation to shareholders to maximize profits by doing away with money losers.

As surprising as it may seem, Avoiding Controversy is something I have seen over and over in my work with companies. And like all of the other barriers, it surfaces at all levels of management. But there are many dynamics at play, as you will find true of each of the eight barriers that we explore.

This one misfire notwithstanding, the COO had a great track record. During his 15 years with the company, he had successfully overseen the integration of several acquisitions. Ironically, they had included having to make some tough decisions about jettisoning unprofitable parts of the business. He was known to be fair-minded and reasonable, which earned him the loyalty not only of his direct reports but of people several levels down in the organization. This middle-market expansion was the COO's blind spot as he had invested much in making it a success—so much that the CEO feared he would lose a key lieutenant if he shut down the project. The CEO made a conscious decision: he rationalized that the disruption caused by losing the COO would be more costly than this money-losing project.

The CEO also realized that shutting down the project could be interpreted as a vote of no confidence in the COO, thus robbing this key player of respect within the organization and possibly compromising his ability to be effective going forward. So while on the surface it looked like the CEO was merely taking the easy way out by not addressing the problem, he believed that it was beneficial for the company to live with this money-losing operation for a while longer. Of course, it was not easy for the rest of the organization to understand why he was doing this.

A publishing company had two analytic units that essentially did the same thing. Each provided market research for the company's extensive prospect mailing program to solicit subscriptions. The analytic units used research and statistics to determine the type of people who would buy a particular type of magazine. They then located appropriate mailing lists and monitored the results. They also created, implemented, and monitored the success of different types of offers (such as buy one, give one free as a gift).

One of the units reported directly into the flagship magazine division. The second unit reported to the centralized marketing division, which supported the other two publishing divisions. This duplication of effort stemmed from a time many years earlier when the central analytic unit did a very poor job of supporting the flagship magazine. As a result, the flagship magazine division created its own unit. Since then the circumstances had changed. An executive who was considered an industry leader was running the central unit, and service levels had increased tremendously. Both heads of their respective divisions now agreed there should only be one group doing analytics, but each believed that his own unit could do the job better. The executive vice president (EVP) to whom both division heads reported did not want to address this issue for fear of demoralizing either team member, each of whom was a high performer. As a result, both analytic units were left untouched— and duplication persisted.

Clearly it would have been far more efficient to have one unit performing the analytics function. But the two executives in charge of the units were fiercely protective of their own units. Neither believed that a new, combined analytics center of excellence should report to the other.

The EVP who oversaw the two divisions didn't want to look like he was favoring one manager over the other. Each of them had a large degree of autonomy and responsibility, and it was important to him that each was in control of his own resources. He knew there should only be one unit, but he didn't want to dictate the answer to them—he wanted them to figure it out for themselves. If he chose a winner, by default there would be a loser. This was a zero-sum game, and the EVP didn't want to demoralize either of his high-performing executives. And he had another concern. One of the potential losers was very close to the EVP's boss, the CEO. If, as a result of his decision, the company lost an executive for whom it had high hopes, the EVP didn't relish the thought of facing the CEO's wrath.

The customer service call center of a bank provided live service 24 hours a day, 7 days a week, as was the industry standard. The head of operations (to whom the call center employees reported) believed that keeping the center open 24/7, 365 days a year was an unnecessary expense. He proposed reducing the hours to 20 a day, shutting down between 1:00 AM and 5:00 AM. This four-hour-a-day reduction would allow him to move from three eight-hour shifts to two ten-hour shifts and would save the bank more than $2 million a year. The retail banking president, whose job it was to keep customers satisfied, resisted the idea of reducing the hours. "We can't offer our customers less service than the competition does," he argued. He believed that customer service was one of the few areas in which the bank could distinguish itself from its competitors. This line of reasoning was behind the retail banking president's already-successful campaign against outsourcing the call center function, as market research had shown that the bank's customers were against outsourcing.

Each executive had a strong argument—substantial cost savings versus keeping up with the competition. The details of the situation were clear and the financials were known, but the two executives couldn't reach an agreement. Neither of them wanted a showdown, and interference on the part of the CEO, to whom both reported, could have been seen as heavy-handedness.

These two departments shared responsibility for numerous initiatives, and they worked closely together and partnered on many other projects. Outside the bank the two executives were best friends, a fact that made it even more surprising that they couldn't reach an agreement on this simple issue. To the retail president, it was clearly important to mirror what competitors were doing. To the head of operations, this was a simple waste of money. This was a highly visible disagreement, and for the CEO the choice was very difficult. Because the debate was so visible to the organization, to side with one executive over the other would clearly undermine the power of whichever executive's suggestion was rejected and potentially cause bitterness in the ranks.

BARING THE BARRIER

You may think the answers to these problems are obvious and that these are just examples of weak managers unable to make decisions. But all three of these companies were considered among the best in their industry. Even the very best managers will have more than a couple of controversial ideas they do not want to act on...and that includes the CEO.

Perhaps they don't want to anger the person they don't agree with, because there is already tension there. Perhaps they don't want to be seen as empowering one person at the expense of another. I even know of one executive who could not bring himself to fire someone who was incompetent at running his division because, frankly, he liked the person too much. Managers are human, after all.

The real reason the Avoiding Controversy barrier exists is because everyone who makes decisions has to pick their battles—whether you have just three people reporting to you or whether you are the CEO in charge of the entire company, you leave some things undecided. That means that issues—often big, controversial issues—are left untouched in every organization.

Sometimes decision makers are essentially powerless. They may have the authority to make a decision, but, from a political perspective, it would make no sense for them to act. To be seen as a manager who wields decision-making authority in anything less than a deft way is to run the risk of being viewed as heavy-handed and unfair. The best managers always think carefully, for example, about a business decision that produces a zero-sum game, where, if there is a winner, there is also a loser. Decisions can become polarizing; people align with one side or the other. Even CEOs can be powerless. True, the CEO is the ultimate boss, but once he or she has designated a person to run a business, unit, or division, for the CEO to intervene would be disrespectful and disruptive. The CEO would be seen to be micromanaging and risk having a revolt on his or her hands. If there is no decision, there is neither a winner nor a loser. So, because of the Avoiding Controversy barrier, contentious matters remain unresolved, because it can seem to make more sense to do nothing.

This is true regardless of whether a manager's style is dictatorial, democratic, or delegating. Even dictators have a power base that they cannot risk offending by issuing a fiat. Democratic bosses, whose teams are accustomed to sharing in the decision making, cannot suddenly switch gears. And bosses who have delegated responsibility run the risk of destroying their power base by taking away authority they have given others.

Another reason that some managers avoid controversy is that they are *deliberately* conflict adverse. I recently had lunch with one of my former client CEOs, and he laid this problem bare. He said, "Some executives will avoid conflict as much as possible as they guide their career through the organization. In my experience, controversy avoiders are often very popular, and it is easy to promote them. Everyone feels good and no one feels threatened when they are promoted. A very successful career path can be built on avoiding controversy."

The best managers know when to pick their battles and have a knack for doing so. But even with deft use of this skill, important issues in the organization are left unaddressed. The examples I have given—most rooted in actual work I have done with companies—are just some ways in which avoiding controversy plays out. One of the reasons a good change process is so successful is that it removes the Avoiding Controversy barrier so that managers no longer have to pick battles; the process does this by shining light on *every* aspect of the company's operations and by forcing the right decision to be made on each one of them.

Now, there are also times that managers do not act for reasons less noble or rational than the situations I have described. Sometimes they do things—or don't do things—because they want to keep people below them from becoming too powerful, for example. But regardless of the reason for the lack of action or not making a decision, and regardless of how a reason might be rationalized, when people avoid dealing with controversy, the barrier is still there and the problems still remain.

BREAKING THE BARRIER

My firm gets hired to break down the barriers in companies and help them achieve change that will make them more efficient, more profitable, and less complex. We do that with the PGI Promise® process, which has proven to be extremely effective in allowing creative ideas to come forward. In most cases in which people are Avoiding Controversy, they are aware that they are doing it. Their motive is to avoid painful consequences. A big part of my work in dealing with the Avoiding Controversy barrier is the creation of a short-term environment in which executives must face issues and must determine the outcome together. Failing that, the CEO must make a decision.

The CEO and other executives are "protected" by the process when making decisions. It provides the ground cover for controversial issues to be resolved and decisions to be made. When the entire organization sees an issue and there is a structure in place to make decisions, it becomes hard to avoid making them. The manager can blame the process: "Sorry—it is the process that is making me decide this." The process also makes it easier for "losers" to accept decisions. And, the fact that there is now a change process in place helps to depersonalize the issue. In fact, every idea is depersonalized—and so is every solution. The *process* is driving the decision making. A key principle of our change process is that ideas are easy to get in the system but hard to take out (see Principle 6 in chapter 9). People have to defend their reasons for *not* doing something. This is the reverse of the way decision making usually takes place. In a typical environment, one person's dissent can be enough to veto a suggestion for change. In the barrier-busting environment, the onus is on a dissenter to say why an idea cannot work.

As a result, the idea becomes focused, and the senior management *has* to make a decision. Attention is focused on the idea. The process forces a decision to be made. The change process forces people to address a controversial issue in a neutral way, armed with facts, as just one of hundreds of decisions that are being made for the improvement of the entire company. In this environment, even the most controversial of ideas must be resolved.

Let us see how the process played out in the three scenarios that we talked about earlier in the chapter.

In the case of the COO's pet project, the process gave him the opportunity to look like he was leading by example by suggesting himself that his midmarket expansion be abandoned. This appeared to be a major sacrifice. And it sent a strong message to the organization: "If I can give up my pet project, I'd better not see you trying to keep yours."

When there is a company-wide review and everything is being considered, it becomes clear that change is going to be occurring on a large scale and that everyone is potentially affected. People are going to have to make sacrifices. I was able to say to the COO, "This is your sacrifice. And if you make that sacrifice—giving up your idea—imagine what a message that's sending to everybody else in the organization." He was able to demonstrate strong leadership; it looked like his decision, he did not have to lose face, and the CEO did not have to risk alienating and losing an important member of his team. And yes, the company saved money by shedding this business in a nondisruptive manner and did not lose the COO.

With the analytic unit, remember, there were two highly qualified, high-performing executives—and no clear reason why one executive's unit should be chosen over the other. It was a simple (but not easy) matter of just having to make a decision that could have seemed arbitrary and clearly would have labeled one a winner and the other a loser.

Ultimately, it did come down to the rather black-or-white decision of Charlie's department being kept rather than Dave's and to combine the units under the centralized marketing division. In this situation, however, Dave was a lot less angry than he would have been because it was done in the context of "it was the right decision for the company" and just one of many being made, some of which made Dave a clear winner. In fact, the process made the decision to lose his analytics unit seem more like a trade-off.

Initially, Dave was not completely happy with the decision to lose analytics for his flagship magazine division, but he stayed with the company—after all, the impartial process ensured that he did not come out labeled a loser. Funnily enough, after a year, he became very enamored with the new centralized unit. The cost savings achieved by eliminating the duplication allowed the new combined unit to afford better technology, which helped Dave do his job better.

The resolution of the call center situation brings to light another important aspect of breaking down barriers—that it is possible for people who have been disagreeing to agree once their perspective shifts.

Now the onus was on the retail president of the bank to say why he did not want to go to a 20-hour call center. It was not up to the operations manager to defend his idea for change. Sure, the retail president had already said that he wanted to do what his competitors were doing. So members of the Catalyst Team (see chapters 9 and 11) asked this simple question: "What's the value of the calls that come in between 1:00 and 5:00 in the morning?" He did not know, so they said, "Okay, well why don't you just go to the call center and check it out? Because if they're saying there's no value in the calls, but you think there is, why don't we all get together in the call center at 1:00 in the morning and see what happens?"

Here the decision was being driven by fact (see Principle 7 in chapter 9: consideration of ideas must be based on facts and analysis, not opinion). And in this case it was easy because the senior executive who was opposing the change in hours, the retail president, actually changed his mind.

He went to sit in a call center for two consecutive mornings between 1:00 and 5:00 and listened to some of the calls that came in. He found that many of the callers were lonely people who wanted someone to talk to or just wanted to see what their balance was. The call center was almost more of a Good Samaritan service than banking customer service! As soon as the retail president recognized this, he had no hesitation in reducing the call center hours.

He was open-minded enough to realize that the calls coming in really were not that valuable in terms of providing excellent customer service, and he was confident enough to be able to change his mind without losing face.

In this case, the process kept the responsibility for resolution firmly in the hands of the heads of retail and operations, with the true onus on the retail president. And this is where it belonged. The process broke the stalemate in this example of the Avoiding Controversy barrier. It forced the responsible parties to make a decision together.

Now, the process cannot take all the credit for this resolution. The retail president was an executive who did not feel threatened when the facts contradicted his belief—and not all executives are as confident or as wise. Some people will argue in spite of the facts. But it is a lot harder to argue in the face of facts—and almost impossible to win when you do.

WHY PEOPLE AVOID CONTROVERSY

BY Dr. Richard Levak

Given human nature, it is hardly surprising that Avoiding Controversy is a hidden barrier to change within companies. Unfortunately, many of us don't know how to successfully navigate controversy, and because it is potentially upsetting, we have many mechanisms to help us avoid dealing with it. This short essay discusses two common mechanisms and describes different personality types and what makes each of them avoid controversy. In reality, the brain is actually hardwired to deal with controversy and its escalation, conflict. Preparing to do battle is part of our evolutionary brain. We are also hardwired to enjoy the endorphin rush of the successful resolution of controversy and conflict. This essay ends with strategies to face and resolve controversy productively.

Controversy is almost inevitable whenever choices exist. In fact, research shows that the more choices there are, the more difficult and controversial the decision making. Controversy in any interaction, when not resolved, can readily turn to conflict. It is the successful resolution of controversy that is a hallmark of a successful marriage, business relationship, or friendship.

But it is not difficult to understand why controversy is avoided. During a controversial interaction, stress hormones are released into the bloodstream. Blood vessels narrow, heart rate goes up, and we prepare to flee or fight. Studies show that even thinking about a controversial topic can significantly raise blood pressure and release stress hormones. These hormones act similarly to steroids, so over time, having constant controversial interactions can break down the body's immune system. Working in a business environment where controversy is avoided may appear to be less stressful.

As humans, we have a number of defenses that inhibit our motivation to confront controversy. They can block and distort reality in such ways that we think we can avoid dealing with controversy. Avoiding controversy can, however, block creativity and potentially evolve into conflict.

Two primary psychological defenses are denial and rationalization.

DENIAL

Denial shields us from admitting unpleasant truths and allows us the comfort of preserving the status quo. Denial usually collapses when things go badly wrong and it becomes clear how obvious the situation actually was.

RATIONALIZATION

Rationalization is another powerful defense protecting us from the discomfort of controversy. Studies on cognitive dissonance show that once we make a difficult decision, we have a tendency to rationalize that it is the best decision we could have made. Consequently, we can avoid controversy by rationalizing to ourselves that we are in fact acting wisely and judiciously, keeping the peace and not being pushy.

In one study, managers were given difficult management choices in which there was no clear answer. Once they made a decision, they argued for its wisdom even though after the experiment new subjects could see the benefits of a different choice. (Once people make a decision, they tend to build a case for it retroactively.) In the case of Avoiding Controversy, many people rationalize the need to get more data or wait and hope the problem resolves itself.

ROLE OF PERSONALITY

People are born with a certain personality type, and experiences shape and enhance it. Three broad personality clusters (among others) are predisposed to Avoiding Controversy.

1. Agreeable Conflict Avoider

On the positive side, Agreeable Conflict Avoiders are consensus builders who have long fuses and go the extra mile to avoid controversy. When they problem-solve, they think about how everybody can win. The downside of this type is that they avoid controversy at the expense of efficiency and sound problem solving.

2. Conscientious, Detail-Oriented, Compulsive Type

On the positive side, these individuals think through decisions carefully, are highly attentive to details, and take their responsibilities seriously. The downside is that they don't want to make a mistake; they are risk avoiders who will avoid controversy for fear that they will be proven wrong and then feel humiliated. They rationalize the need for more data and time before making decisions.

3. Sensitive Type

The positive side of the Sensitive type is an ability to fit in and play the right role in different situations and to be vigilant to keep things on track. However, the negative side is that Sensitive types can make mountains out of molehills, hold grudges, and overreact in crises.

Regardless of personality type, people find Avoiding Controversy easier than dealing with it. For that reason, we have evolved rituals and rules of behavior, such as etiquette, to minimize controversy.

At the same time, humans are wired to feel the reward of successful controversy resolution. When a controversy is successfully resolved, the endorphins that are released into the bloodstream lead to pleasurable positive emotions that promote human bonding. Research shows that teams that resolve controversy successfully become bonded, creative, and loyal to one another. However, people need a structure that can help them manage controversy. If they can be made to feel safe and rewarded for seeing new and creative ways of doing things, they will want to do so. Fear, whether of looking foolish or of creating controversy, creates tunnel vision.

The change process outlined in this book, the PGI Promise®, encourages people to identify controversy, highlight it, and resolve it with fact-based analysis. If people are encouraged to do so in a safe and transparent environment, they will work hard to contribute and experience the endorphin rush that comes from successfully resolving controversy.

IT IS NOT JUST CEOS

Controversial ideas are not just the domain of the C suite. Every manager has to make decisions about what ideas he or she is going to act on, often employing, on a smaller scale, the same mental gymnastics as the CEO. The person who makes controversial decisions may well be doing the right things for the company but could lose a lot of influential friends in the process.

While the CEO and other senior managers likely will know about the big ideas with the largest potential for financial impact, they will not be aware of ones farther down the line. But other managers will. When you add the impact of the big ideas at the top of the pyramid with the impact of the countless ones farther down, you can see that unwillingness and inability to deal with controversial ideas is costing your company a great deal of money.

THE BARRIER IN BRIEF

TAKEAWAY: Controversial ideas exist and issues are left unresolved because dealing with them would cause too much disruption. Politics, personalities, alliances, and appearances are all factors in why controversy is avoided. Usually these ideas for change have surfaced within a company over and over again because they resolve obvious problems and the issues are often large and strategic.

SOLUTION: Neutralize controversial ideas by making the resolution part of a larger process for change that is not about any one person or project.

LOOK AT YOUR ORGANIZATION

- What are some ideas that you have seen scuttled or that just aren't being dealt with because they would be too disruptive?
- What suggestions have you been afraid to make?
- What ideas have you rejected for being "too controversial"?

CHAPTER 2

BARRIER 2:
POOR USE OF TIME

IN THE EARLY 1980S, HARVARD BUSINESS SCHOOL attracted outstanding students from all over the world. For the 700 students who enrolled each year, it was not only a highly competitive environment but also an exciting learning experience when friendships were built for life.

One of my key life lessons came from my time on campus. The case study is the predominant teaching method at HBS. It involves studying two or three 20- to 30-page "cases" each evening to prepare for classes the next day. Classes are taught in sections of about 90 students in a theater setting, with the professor serving as the moderator of a discussion about the case. One of the key ways students' performance is measured is by class participation; getting air time in a group of 90 students is no easy task. In every class, the professor asks one student at random to "open" the case, which involves describing the circumstances and the problem. This is the student's chance to shine—or to fail—and because of the numbers of students, you have the chance to open a case only once in each class. If you did not prepare the previous evening and you are called on, your grade is shot.

My biggest problem wasn't in being underprepared—it was in sometimes being late for class. A couple of friends and I had volunteered to host a study group early every morning to help struggling students. We wanted to be absolutely sure they were well prepared, so we took advantage of every minute we had. Now I certainly don't think that was a poor use of my time. Where my time-management problem came in was that I often felt the need for a caffeine boost after the early study group. There was just enough time before class to dash to the cafeteria to get a coffee—unless there was a long line. I wouldn't know that until I got there—with the result that it was sometimes a challenge to get to class on time. My sectionmates good-humoredly kidded me about it. One day, in my penultimate class, our professor, Ted, told us that we had no overnight reading because we would use the final class to prepare for the exam. The next day I showed up ten minutes late, thanks to my coffee run, and crept quietly into my customary seat in the "Sky Deck"—the back row of the lecture hall.

Much to my surprise, given Ted's usual punctuality, the class had not yet started. Ted launched the final class by saying, "Now, it's our very last case of the year, and since it's your last chance to impress me, I'm sure you all came well prepared, and I'd like to kick off strongly. Let me see—who can I get to open? Neil, how about you?"

I was mortified. What happened to using the class to prepare for the exam? And I had already opened several weeks ago. My friend Alberto, seated next to me, discreetly pushed over his study notes. Following them closely, I ad-libbed for about a minute. I had just made, with supreme confidence, what I thought was a very good point when the entire class burst into laughter. There was no case; the entire class, led by Ted and Alberto, had conspired against me.

Ted was a wonderful professor—he didn't count my chronic lateness against me and in fact used it to help teach me a very valuable lesson about my use of time. As an undergrad, I was dedicated and hardworking, and I was able to graduate without having to think about any of my natural work habits. But in my first year at HBS, Ted helped me become aware of how poorly I was managing my time. You never know how Poor Use of Time will come back to haunt you, and since that time I have become very conscious of how important it is to use and manage time properly. This experience enabled me to correct a behavior (management of time) early in my career, but it also made me recognize that time is an important ingredient to success. And it is something that most managers overlook.

(Alberto, by the way, went on to become one of the early practitioners of private equity in Europe, effectively retiring before he was 50.)

Of the eight barriers described in this book, Poor Use of Time is unique because it has three distinct aspects. There is management of time, which is a matter of individual choice; use of time, which is a function of company processes; and the value of time, which is a lack of appreciation about the value of time to others. This barrier is unique in that it has a behavioral component and a structural component, and it also has another component: how others value time.

We learned in the introduction to this book about the difference between behavioral and structural barriers. My lateness for class was due to management of time—the behavioral part of the barrier. If my board required me to spend hours documenting my conversations with potential clients, that time requirement would be about "use of time." Under that scenario, because how my time is spent—or at least a portion of it—is dictated by company policy, that is structural.

The demands of customers—appreciation of the value of time—is the third driver of how time is poorly spent. This appreciation (or the lack of it) can force different choices about how priorities are organized to serve the customer. Here the choice of how time is spent is not influenced by the individual or the company but rather by the requirements of the customer. But the company does have the opportunity to charge more money for services done under certain time constraints—which helps the company to be rewarded for the "value of time."

HOW POOR USE OF TIME FORCES COMPANIES TO DO DUMB THINGS

An investment firm gave its customers the option of getting their monthly statements online only, as part of the firm's "going green" initiative. When the company saw that more than 30 percent of its customers chose to get their statements electronically, it expected to reduce complexity and improve customer service while also saving money. After all, the company would be printing, processing, and mailing about a third fewer statements. Yet six months later, senior management realized the company was spending just as much money on monthly statements as it had been before it made the switch to electronic statements.

The investment firm never stopped printing, processing, or mailing the statements. Instead, to satisfy customers who no longer wanted printed statements, it resorted to a simple fix: it just changed the customers' mailing addresses to its own headquarters, where the statements were destroyed after they arrived in the mail. What would cause a company to do something such as this, which on the surface seems incredibly "dumb"?

Allowing statements to be viewed online was relatively simple to do, but to stop customer statement delivery required a system-wide reprogramming. Getting that fix made would take a lot of time and would mean adjusting priorities. The technology department had all the information it needed to make the change; it knew what had to be done, it knew the savings that would come with the change, and it knew how important the change was to the customer—but it just didn't have time to do it without shifting other important priorities. A senior manager in the technology department figured out that a "simple" temporary fix was just to go in and change to the company's own headquarters the addresses of customers who did not want paper statements. The real problem was not solved, because of "management of time" in the technology department.

In the meantime, not a penny was saved... and the green initiative was not helped.

When managers decide they don't have time to do something, the decision is not a matter of benign neglect. Poor prioritizing is an example of the behavioral aspect of the Poor Use of Time barrier and means some important things do not get done. That, in turn, means problems are left unfixed. In this case, it wasn't even a matter of people spending time to figure out a solution. The technology department knew what had to be done, and that made the lack of action seem almost deliberately neglectful.

All food manufacturers have new-product departments, which are responsible for researching, developing, and testing the recipes for new food items. One option for companies is to extend food brands by taking a core item and adjusting the recipe to create what seems like a new, different product. A recently hired marketing executive was pushing one food company to branch out beyond the traditional ice cream flavors it was known for. He came back from an overseas trip waxing lyrical about the honey and ginger ice cream he had tasted while abroad and suggested that the company create its own version. The new-products department went to work, creating and trying various recipes.

After months of trial and error, the department finally settled on a receipe that was a subtle and delicious blend of these two distinct flavors. Very pleased with the outcome, the marketing executive organized a taste-testing day for senior staff. "This is great," said one vice president who had been with the company a long time. "It tastes exactly the same as it did when we first came up with it. I'm glad we're finally getting around to marketing it."

It turned out that the company had produced this exact flavor a dozen years earlier, having copied it from the overseas market, but had considered it too "exotic." Since then, the staff in the research department had all left the company, taking with them all the information about what had been previously tried and tested and the results of those tests. The company lacked any way to retain institutional knowledge once employees left. This was especially wasteful considering that a certain level of recipe development work serves as a foundation for creating other recipes. But because there was no way to capture it, the department was constantly starting from the very beginning with every new product. The research that was done was incredibly valuable, even if a product had failed. It was good to know what had worked and what had not so that the researchers did not have to start from scratch in devising every new product.

I see duplication of effort in every organization—two departments or units providing essentially the same function, such as at the publishing company we wrote about in chapter 1. But what was happening at the food manufacturer is different—it is *repetition* of effort, which is almost always unnecessary, particularly when the same group or division is doing the work over again. Here time was being used very poorly, and the time in the new product department was particularly valuable. As soon as one project was finished, the next began, as there was a waiting list for new product experiments to start.

Unless material facts change, there is every reason to take advantage of work that has already been done. Every company has a foundation of knowledge. But when that knowledge is not shared—or when people are not aware of its existence—the wheel gets reinvented. This is an example of how the structural aspect of the Poor Use of Time barrier is at play. Employees are not able to go back to use information from tests that have been done in the past, which they should do when they are thinking about new items or new ideas.

Package delivery companies are obsessed (understandably so) with time and volume—they want to deliver the greatest number of packages in the least amount of time possible. The local routing manager of one delivery company was not impressed when one driver suggested adding an extra eight miles to his daily route. The driver persuaded his manager to let him try. That day the driver returned to the depot 15 minutes earlier than usual. The manager was intrigued. If all drivers could duplicate this time savings, the company could get far more packages delivered far more quickly.

The simple change the driver made was in doing away with as many left-hand turns as he could. He changed his delivery route so it was composed of as many right turns as possible. Then he could take advantage of right turns on red; no longer did he have to wait for red lights to turn green or wait for breaks in traffic to make left turns. Although this change added eight miles to his route, the time saved making deliveries more than compensated for the extra mileage (and extra gas) used. This is another example of the structural aspect of the Poor Use of Time barrier—of a company not using its employees' time as well as it can.

The wire transfer department of a bank opened daily at 8:00 AM but had a cutoff time of 3:00 PM for customers to issue wiring instructions so that a funds transfer could be completed that day. Every day, the department was deluged with requests for transfers between 2:00 PM and the 3:00 PM deadline. Some 60 percent of all transfers were done in that last frantic hour, with the result that very little work was done in the first six hours the department was open. This created huge problems in terms of staffing the department. In the morning, staff members were underutilized and sat around waiting for work to do. In the hour between 2:00 PM and 3:00 PM, they were run off their feet, which also increased their chances of making a mistake. The bank wanted to encourage customers to spread out their wire transfer requests over the course of the day to even out the work flow and solve their staffing problem, so it decided to double the price for transfers done between 2:00 PM and 3:00 PM.

The results were surprising. Instead of seeing a redistribution of the time the transfer requests came in, very few customers changed their habits—they simply paid the increased fee. The customers' own internal processes were geared up to transfer funds toward the end of the day, and they didn't want to change their processes. The wire transfer department saw its profits increase by 30 percent. The bank discovered that from the customers' perspective, it was doing more than just transferring funds. It was providing a service with a time-based value—and customers were willing to pay for the value of time.

BARING THE BARRIER

MANAGEMENT OF TIME

"I don't have the time to do that right now" is one of the most common reasons given for why something does not get done. And it is also one of the worst. You cannot create time—but you can *find* time for important activities.

In fairness, your colleagues are likely telling the truth when they say they do not have time to do something. Excellent companies are not filled with people who have spare time on their hands to use as items come up and new jobs need to be done. At any given moment, employees have lots of projects and people competing for their attention, all of which have to be prioritized. Ideally, employees make their decisions based on what they believe is best for the organization, but (as with other behavioral barriers) they don't always get that right. Consequently, very often they make poor decisions about how they manage their time.

In the best organizations, bosses don't micromanage their employees. Managers cannot—and should not—manage every single decision, and they need to be able to trust workers to make good decisions about how they allocate their time. This kind of freedom and autonomy makes people's jobs rewarding, challenging, and interesting, and employers benefit when people are engaged in their work. However, a frequent by-product of workers having freedom is Poor Use of Time. In making their own decisions, people can become disconnected from the priorities of other parts of the organization—or even their own department.

So here is the paradox: managers are given autonomy so they can make their own decisions, but that very autonomy can rob them of the support, guidance, and information they need to make the best decisions for the organization.

> One of the things that happens when a project like the PGI Promise® starts is that people suddenly find the time to do all those things they just did not have time for. Knowing that there will be scrutiny does amazing things in terms of motivating people.

Without this organizational support, people often make decisions that are in their own best interests (or around what happens to interest them). They do not do this subversively—people are not making poor decisions for the wrong reasons. But this is yet another area where human nature kicks in. Think about the upcoming weekend. Would you prefer to pay your bills or watch your daughter's soccer game? People tend to do those tasks they enjoy doing before doing those they have to do. They procrastinate. At work, they may get their organizational priorities wrong. In the absence of guidance and information, they may not be able to do any better. So, "I don't have time" can be a default response for "I chose to do the wrong things with my time."

WHY PEOPLE PROCRASTINATE

By *Dr. Richard Levak*

Procrastination is a basic human impulse that is as old as civilization itself. Human nature, driven by the twin desires to seek pleasure and avoid pain, is vulnerable to short-term self-interest and self-defeating behavior. Procrastination displays both of these attributes. It is pretty easy to predict that procrastination will show up as a hidden behavioral barrier in companies.

Procrastination involves an area of the brain called the prefrontal cortex, where executive functioning is located. This area of the brain keeps our daily lives organized and on track. Executive functioning can vary naturally, just like math ability. Some of us resolve to do a task and naturally fail to regulate the interruptions. We state a mission but we don't motivate ourselves to get going. Although many people procrastinate, research shows that 20 percent of people are chronic procrastinators.

Our individual level of anxiety also plays a role in why we procrastinate. A certain amount of anticipatory anxiety is necessary to keep us on track in all that we do. Most people feel mild levels of anxiety with a deadline looming, and that serves as motivation. But people with low levels of anxiety don't get the same "signals," so they tend to be most productive only when they have so much to do that finally a "motivating" level of anxiety kicks in. These people do best when given strict deadlines with a number of concrete milestones along the way to keep them motivated.

Others with low levels of anxiety need the adrenaline that comes with doing something they perceive as pleasurable or exciting. When faced with the need to perform activities that won't produce adrenaline, they decide they "don't have time" for them. Those people need a framework to be able to assess the value of completing a task, regardless of how "unsexy" it feels.

Other people have the opposite problem: higher-than-average levels of anxiety. They are prone to self-doubt and second-guessing. These individuals suffer from "analysis paralysis," collecting increasing amounts of data and avoiding difficult decisions as long as possible. They "don't have time" because a decision is "difficult" so they busy themselves with real but less-relevant tasks and decisions. Like those who need adrenaline, they also need a framework to assess the value of a particular decision.

Procrastination is partly driven by recognition of the immediacy of unpleasant hard work versus an inability to connect to the distant reward for completing it. Research shows that open-ended tasks in the future are easier to postpone than short-term concrete projects. The more ill-defined the task and the farther it is in the future, the less likely it is to get done.

A study revealed that forcing people to problem-solve using concrete small steps increased their completion rate of unrelated tasks. Consciously being in the habit of getting things done increases the chances that you will get other things done. Decision making is like a muscle that has to be exercised. Setting concrete practical goals decreases procrastination and increases productivity. Quantifying the results of delay encourages people to take action and also makes them accountable in very concrete ways.

While procrastination is about the individual, there are things a manager and a company can do to help break the propensity to procrastinate. Shedding light on the decisions that need to be made and holding people responsible for those decisions decreases procrastination, particularly if people feel they won't be unduly judged or criticized.

Here are some other suggestions for helping people get past procrastination:

- Whenever possible, break tasks down into manageable, concrete components, with interim milestones that can be measured. If possible, limit options in order to make the scope of a task less daunting.

- Develop an analytical framework that quantifies the savings over time (or the cost of delay in completing the task) in order to prioritize outstanding tasks most efficiently.
- Reward personnel for timely completion of tasks, so that it becomes part of the company culture.
- Develop a mechanism for public follow-up so neglected efforts can be identified. A crucial role of meetings is that they spur participants to complete their work in advance of the meeting. No one wants to look bad in front of others.

USE OF TIME

Looking at how companies use their people's time is complex. It is safe to assume that excellent companies do not knowingly waste their employees' time. But I find examples of wasted time in every company I work with.

The most common example is repetition of effort—work that has already been done once being done a second time. Companies continuously repeat tasks that they have already done. It is very evident in the new-product research example. Every company has a foundation of knowledge, whether it is institutional knowledge or new research. But if the knowledge and information are not recorded or not available, they cannot be transferred or leveraged.

I see repetition in many different ways all across companies. Sometimes it is more deliberate. In quality-control areas, there are often checkers checking the checkers. This repetitive activity is particularly common in industries that are government regulated, such as banking or pharmaceuticals. Today banks typically have many duplicative controls that look at organizational risks. This is done because banks do not want to make bad loans, just as health-care companies do not want to release bad drugs. But the checks are often frustrating to those employees on the front line who recognize that many of the checks are unnecessary. They do not reduce risk to any measurable degree; instead, they merely serve to give management (or in some cases regulators) extra comfort.

Sometimes (as in the case of the delivery company) it is not apparent that time is being wasted until someone comes along with a bright idea and is able to show how much time can be saved. Deciding if time is being spent in the absolute best way possible requires genuine creativity and some commitment to experimentation. Every possible time variable needs to be examined and questioned. For a company, deciding how time could be better spent is much more subtle than for an individual; the signs are not always obvious, and the solutions are not always intuitive. Who would have believed that adding eight miles to a route could save a driver time?

VALUE OF TIME

The last aspect of time has to do with the value assigned to it, and often that value is zero—your colleagues may not appreciate the value that time has to the customer. The wire-transfer department was hoping that a price change would alter customer behavior. Instead, it learned that customers placed a high value on time and were willing to pay for it.

Some companies and industries do a better job of charging for time than others. There is a reason that airlines charge you even higher penalties to change your flights at the last minute—and that people are willing to spend four or five times as much for the flexibility of a same-day ticket as it would have cost had it been booked earlier. At least one computer company has a "premium" service line that means callers will not have to wait to be connected to a tech specialist to help them fix their computer. And, of course, the company charges a premium for that service. To some customers, their time (and quickly removing their frustration) is more important than money.

Other companies and industries are terrible at charging for the value of time. If your cable company could guarantee you that a worker would get to your home in a 90-minute window instead of forcing you to stay home from work to accommodate the four- to eight-hour slot it customarily offers, wouldn't you be willing to pay extra for that?

Ultimately, for a company, the value of time comes down to what it thinks customers are willing to pay for. Paying for time should not seem like a penalty to the customer. One credit card company had the idea of charging its customers $5 to avoid waiting on hold to get a problem resolved. Perhaps they got this idea from the computer company just described. But the aggressive feedback from consumers, all of it recorded, quickly made the company change its mind. Many calls were related to wrong card charges. Customers were more than a little annoyed to have to pay to more quickly resolve a problem that was not their fault in the first place. In this case, the company quickly decided that it was not a good idea to charge customers to solve a problem caused by product use.

BREAKING THE BARRIER

You know the saying, It takes money to make money? Well, it also takes time to "make" time—or at least to break the Poor Use of Time barrier. And this is another paradox. It is hard to step back to figure out whether time is being used well because you need to make time to do it.

To break the Poor Use of Time barrier, managers need to continuously reassess how they spend their time and whether they have their time priorities right. Companies need to assess why employees think they lack time and what is not getting done as a result of their beliefs and choices; companies must also look at how they demand that their employees use their time; and finally, they must ensure that they place the appropriate monetary value on the special time requirements of their customers.

> People say they cannot find the time to do things, yet they always find the time to fix things when they break. Companies need to create that sense of urgency *before* a problem occurs.

Managers can become very defensive, because how they spend their time seems very personal to them. Human nature causes people not to react well when they are told they have their priorities wrong. They do not like to think they are making poor choices. And time is typically one of the very few things at work that employees have control over. If a boss impinges on this freedom, it is not likely to be well received.

Part of the value of a good process to remove barriers is that it sheds a very public light on areas and issues that might otherwise remain hidden or ignored. While that is a help in breaking down all the barriers, it is especially the case with the Poor Use of Time barrier. For one thing, you will be amazed at how quickly people find time when they know that change is afoot. Whenever companies announce that a project is starting, there is always a flurry of activity because people do not want to be embarrassed in front of their team, their boss, or the chief executive with the things they did not find time for. Things that should have been done quickly get done. So part of breaking this barrier is simply putting a spotlight on it.

Getting people past "I don't have the time" is about motivating people on an individual level and getting them to think differently about the way they decide to prioritize their time. It is not about micromanaging them. And it is also about making them aware of, or reinforcing, organizational priorities. When your colleagues have this information and support, they are equipped to continue to determine their individual priorities but to align them better with the company's priorities.

By contrast, changing the way people *use* their time is more complicated, because the root of the problem lies in organizational processes, not people.

A good change process not only roots out all cases of duplicative or repetitive activities but also questions the true value and need of all activities while also measuring their cost. And part of the challenge to a company is recognizing that time is very valuable; how can the organization make better use of it? Are there creative ideas, which may not be intuitively obvious, about how time is used and how it can be better used? Every company has a foundation of knowledge; yet not every company has formalized the collection and accessibility of it. Companies can do a better job of institutionalizing knowledge, and that's one of the things that a good process helps to put in place or encourage.

When assigning the proper value to time, companies need to ask two questions:

1. What are we doing (or what could we be doing) that is time sensitive and that customers would value?
2. How do our customers value their own time? If we could save time for them, is that something they would pay for?

When the CEO at the investment house found out—to his ire—that the monthly statements were still being sent out (and to his firm's own address, no less), getting the programming fix done was as simple as making sure people knew he was annoyed. They needed to make the time to fix the problem, and they had to recognize that they had their priorities wrong. Sometimes a fix is that simple, because the problem itself is fairly simple.

The food manufacturer I worked with decided to create a "recipe library." It organized all its recipes and made them available, so each time a product was being considered and developed, researchers then knew how much preliminary work had already been done on that kind of product or its ingredients. It didn't matter whether the product had been successful—the efforts were recorded. After the recipe library was instituted, the researchers spent far less time in developing new products when an element of them had been tried before. Less time meant less cost. And there was another advantage: the time to market new products—very important in the food industry—was also dramatically reduced as new products came to rely on old research. The concept was also applied to other aspects of food research, working equally well for packaging design and for product manufacturing.

The local routing manager of the transportation company liked his driver's no-left-turns idea so much that he instituted it across his entire fleet of trucks. This allowed him to have fewer trucks on the road (as each truck now could deliver more packages), and it also allowed for quicker delivery to customers. After the program was instituted, another huge advantage was revealed: one of the greatest causes of road accidents is a truck turning left across traffic. An extra bonus was a 25 percent reduction in traffic accidents as a direct result of fewer left turns.

The wire-transfer department did not get the result it expected—but it got one that was more than acceptable: a 30 percent boost in profits. Customers were happy to pay a higher price if they could do things when they wanted to. The extra profits allowed the department to staff itself more adequately for the "rush" hour and still charge a healthy premium over the standard price it continued to charge customers for using non-peak hours. And because the final hour was now better staffed and less frantic, the company found another hidden benefit: fewer mistakes by employees transferring funds during that hour.

THE BARRIER IN BRIEF

TAKEAWAY: Even in organizations where people are very busy and long days are the norm, employees use their time very poorly. There are three aspects to Poor Use of Time: you and your colleagues do not have the time to do things ("the management of time"); companies use their employees' time very poorly ("the use of time"); and time isn't valued appropriately ("the value of time").

SOLUTION: When breaking the Poor Use of Time barrier, the first aspect is addressed by changing the way people think and behave. Changing processes addresses the second aspect. Assigning a monetary value to time—something that is often missed—addresses the third aspect.

LOOK AT YOUR ORGANIZATION
MANAGEMENT OF TIME

- What projects do you not have time for?
- What are you doing instead of those projects?
- What are the implications—for your department and others—of your choices?

USE OF TIME

- In what areas is your company reinventing the wheel?
- Where does institutional knowledge reside?
- What could be done differently that would allow people to do more in the same amount of time?

VALUE OF TIME

- Are there services for which your company should charge more because the customer values timely delivery of those services?
- Do you think there are services your customers would pay more for because of the value of *their* own time?

CHAPTER 3

BARRIER 3: RELUCTANCE TO CHANGE

AT THE AGE OF 16, WHILE STILL AT SCHOOL, I HAD two part-time jobs. My schoolmates thought one of the jobs was very cool: I was the assistant projectionist at the local cinema, which allowed me to get in to watch R-rated movies. I became very popular as my friends were dying to know about movies that we were not able to see, but in truth I never actually got to watch them.

Frank, the projectionist, was very proud that he had been doing the same job for more than 30 years. In those days there were two huge arc-lamp projectors in the projection room, and each would alternately show 20 minutes of a movie. The real skill was in the changeover—closing the window to one projector at the same time as opening the window to the other—and this was a two-man job.

The job was physically grueling; not only did the projectors give off an immense amount of heat, but every 20 minutes a reel of film had to be replaced in one of the projectors. The reels came in canisters that were some 18 inches across and weighed more than 50 pounds. Every 20 minutes we had to let the projector cool down, remove the old reel of film, carry it down to the basement, bring the next reel up from the basement, and intricately thread the new reel through the hot projector so that it would be ready to go. For the average movie, this could happen six or seven times. You can guess who was assigned the task of running up and down with the heavy canisters. There was no time to watch the movie.

One day I had a brain wave. There was space to stack two piles of canisters in the projection room. What if I brought them all up before the movie started and took them all down at the end? Not only would this mean there would be more time and less stress between reel changes, it also meant I could actually watch the movie. With much delight I announced to Frank that I would do this. Frank's face slowly turned to a deep purple hue; he was outraged. For the next five minutes he went into a tirade that included words and phrases such as "unprofessionalism," "straight out of school," and "taking shortcuts." I knew from that moment on that the budding career as a projectionist that Frank was envisioning for me was finished.

I had learned my first lesson about the Reluctance to Change barrier. When someone's way of doing things is threatened by an idea from another person, they resist the suggestion. Logic and common sense are not behind the resistance; there are other factors at work.

This is perhaps the easiest of the eight barriers to understand and immediately identify with. We are all creatures of habit. When I come home from work in the evening, I always sit in the same spot on the sofa, and woe betides the son or daughter who sits in my spot at the dinner table. When it is time for a new car, I tend to go for the same make, even though it might make more sense to choose a different model, and I always buy the car instead of considering something wholly different, such as leasing it. We all like to do things that we know how to do and that make us feel good. You have heard the phrase, "If it's not broken, why fix it?" If we like something and it works well for us, why change it?

> Fear of the unknown is a large component of people's Reluctance to Change. Make the process as transparent as possible, and encourage employees to share their fears.

People also resist change because they do not know exactly what the change will mean to them. Often it is difficult to predict the full outcome of what will happen when change has been implemented. The memory of unexpected, unpleasant results from previous changes can drive fear of change. The greatest cause of stress is uncertainty about the future. Fear of the unknown is at the root of this uncertainty. So, even if a change produces a superb end result and a far better outcome than anticipated, the *process of change* itself is very stressful.

WHY PEOPLE ARE RELUCTANT TO CHANGE

By *Dr. Richard Levak*

From a human behavior point of view, you would expect to find that Reluctance to Change is a natural barrier in every organization. For many years it was accepted wisdom that employees would naturally resist change. Yet research reveals that people will embrace change if

- They see the logic behind it.
- They feel they have control over its onset and evolution.
- They see it as nonthreatening and self-esteem enhancing.
- The change has the possibility of future benefits to them.

People embrace change more readily if they feel they can try it on step by step, making adjustments as things progress.

Conversely, they resist change if they don't see the benefits, feel it is pushed on them, have no control over the process, and perceive that it threatens their well-being with uncertain future consequences. Research also shows that people will accept change up to a certain point of novelty. Beyond that point, as novelty increases, people feel threatened, so their willingness to change decreases.

Resistance to new insights and to change in general is a primary defense mechanism. It occurs because of the way our brain organizes information. Just as a computer has an operating system in which information is organized along certain predictable categories, so, too, our brain promotes order by creating rules by which we categorize data. It's a way to avoid having to think too much and allows us to operate on automatic pilot for periods of time. Changing a set of habits or having to learn a new language or set of rules costs us effort and energy. In a new situation, we can no longer work on cruise control. We have to pay attention.

The more complex and uncertain the change, the more fear and anxiety people experience and the greater the resistance. Consequently people resist big changes more than small, incremental ones. Insecurity about assimilating the new skills involved in change and fears about increasing workload demands also create resistance.

Personality also plays a part in people's openness to change. Some people like to experiment and actually need the excitement of novelty. Sometimes they create change without careful thought and due diligence because they need it to feel the adrenaline rush of living on the edge. When such people control companies, sometimes they go on merger and acquisition binges or expand into new products and territories for ego gratification and change for its own sake.

Other personality types are resistant to change, needing the predictability of sameness to manage their anxiety and fears of unpredictable catastrophe. Most people are in the middle, quick to argue for predictable sameness unless they can be persuaded to see the benefits of change to the organization and themselves.

People prefer to learn vicariously about behaviors that are potentially dangerous rather than risk finding out firsthand. Before I take a risk with change, I may ask others how they feel about it. Negative viewpoints can quickly become exaggerated and overgeneralized, leading to cohesive group resistance. Preempting resistance through early education and communication to help people understand the logic and mutual benefits behind change is a crucial part of the process. Change is also more acceptable if it is compatible with the existing values and experiences of the people being asked to change.

HOW DOES CHANGE OCCUR?

People will expend the energy to make changes if they perceive a benefit to the organization and/or themselves. That people will change for an altruistic motive is well documented, as is the case with the conservation movement. Employees are not purely self-interested resistors of change. They will make changes if they are recognized for doing so and if the change makes a difference to the company. People are more likely to accept change if it is clearly understood and concrete. For example, telling all call center agents to be more gracious to customers is not as effective as telling them to say, "Good morning, how are you?"

Change is more likely to be long lasting if a reward closely follows the changed behavior. Immediacy of positive feedback is the best predictor that a particular behavior change will stick. To effectively shape change-oriented behavior, managers need to catch people doing the right thing and verbally reward them.

When introducing change in an organization, make an effort to communicate early on the rationale and benefits of the change, addressing concerns workers may have, especially about their role in the future, job security, and so on. When possible, break the change down into steps or increments so they can be assimilated more easily. Be sure to recognize people for responding and reward them for incorporating the changes. Remember that individual responses will differ depending on an individual's personality, and some people are naturally more cautious than others.

It takes courage to change. Altering comfortable habits combined with the stress caused by uncertainty and fear of the unknown mean that change is not natural to most people. Due to people's natural tendency to avoid stress and the unknown, the Reluctance to Change barrier arises.

For a company, this reluctance proves quite a challenge. Most companies need to think about change constantly so they can stay ahead of their competitors, whether it is bringing out a new product line or simply modifying a process that helps provide better customer service. A workforce with a natural Reluctance to Change presents a real problem for companies. Ideas are abandoned or forgotten, and the company becomes a follower rather than a leader in the marketplace. If it does not keep up with the changing needs of customers, the company will lose clients and put the organization at risk. The Reluctance to Change barrier leaves a lot of unidentified opportunities and unfulfilled ideas in every company.

HOW RELUCTANCE TO CHANGE FORCES COMPANIES TO DO DUMB THINGS

In places where electricity runs through overhead wires rather than underground, trees are a major problem when wind or storms cause branches to fall into the wires, resulting in short circuits. Customers lose electricity, and utility repair crews have to go out to fix the problem. To prevent this from happening, maintenance crews—who are often called linemen—cut down branches when they grow too close to utility lines.

One utility one of my colleagues worked with had a schedule in which the maintenance department trimmed trees across the whole system on a three-year cycle—every day the crews would visit a different area to cut branches—whether the branches needed trimming or not. There was no direction about where the crews would go based on need; they visited a certain area based on when they had last been there.

The system worked reasonably well, considering that one of the key factors was the weather—highly unpredictable and completely uncontrollable. But some years earlier, two linemen had an idea to change the process. They suggested that two of them should do nothing but walk the system, covering the whole line in the space of a year. It wouldn't be their job to do the repairs; they would just do inspections and mark any trees or branches that needed cutting. They would then call in the maintenance crew to do just the work that needed to be done. This change in process had lots of advantages. It would mean that the entire line would be inspected every year instead of every three years. It would result in fewer outages as problem branches would be caught more quickly. It would be more environmentally friendly; crews could wait a year to see if a branch was likely to become a problem. It would also please customers, as their trees would be trimmed as needed, not every three years. And, most important, it would mean 60 percent fewer linemen, as fewer branches would be cut.

The linemen's manager thought this was a great idea, and he was not a "Management Blocker" (see chapter 5). But two years later, the idea still had not been implemented. There was never any pressure on the manager to change the process, which worked well enough. He had schedules and rosters worked out, he had a routine that ran like clockwork, and he had a happy crew who knew where they would be working over the coming months, as the three-year cycle scarcely changed.

In the retail store environment—a fast-moving industry—it is important to transmit sales and pricing data electronically to headquarters on a daily basis. Doing this allows decisions to be made about several things critical to the business: what inventory to order in advance so the stores do not run out, what prices to change if a new item either flies off the shelf or does not sell as expected, and which items should be placed on sale immediately to clear inventory. It also allows information about how sales are being affected when a competitor tries something new in a market. Immediate sales and product information is key to managing the business. This data is so critical that one company carried two separate telephone lines, each with a different carrier, feeding each of its retail stores. The second line was considered a backup. But the chain continued to struggle transmitting the data from all its stores on a daily basis. Every week all the lines to at least one of its stores (and often more) went down. Inconsistent data collection was impacting the company's ability to manage the business. Why was it happening?

Most power outages to stores were caused by construction accidents that damaged the cable carrying the lines. As most lines, even from different carriers, go through the same cable, the second backup line was often damaged at the same time as the primary line, so the insurance proved useless. Several people within the organization had discussed using a wireless system as the backup rather than a physical line, but the communications manager had not made the change. He didn't see the need to change because the company had created an internal estimating system, a Band-Aid if you will, to make up for the lack of data when lines went down. "We've made it work," he insisted. "Besides, wireless will have its own set of problems. We could go to a lot of trouble and expense and not be any better off."

The communications manager's Reluctance to Change was a combination of complacency—everyone had learned to live with this less-than-ideal situation—and a fear of the unknown. The manager's previous experience with changing systems made him less than enthusiastic about doing so again. What problems would wireless bring? What new adaptations would a switch to wireless demand?

In almost every technology environment I have worked with, the bottom 5 percent of programmers are not just less productive but actually cause problems. Their ineffectual work causes mistakes that create work for the top 10 percent of the group—those with the skill to diagnose and fix problems. And programming is an area in which even one simple mistake in a line of code can have devastating consequences. Enterprise-wide systems and processes can be shut down or delayed, which is costly and frustrating to both employees and customers. Yet, time and again, I have also found that while the problem is well known—and the solution painfully obvious—nothing is done about it. It may cause more work to keep on the laggards, but it's also simpler than making a change.

In one bank, this issue became very apparent while I was working there. The company website, which was used by many customers, went down twice in a matter of weeks. This was so visible it made big news, much to the embarrassment of the chief executive and senior management. In the first instance, the company ran into capacity issues that it thought had already been addressed. The second time around, problems were associated with an upgrade; despite months of work, the upgrade failed. In both cases, junior programmers had worked on the projects. The work had not been considered difficult, which was why it was delegated to junior staff. Yet the mistakes made were both highly visible and catastrophic. When the website went down, all resources were diverted to fix it, causing other projects to go off schedule.

This is a classic case of it *is* broke, but it will take me some effort to fix it and it may not be worth the effort. In this instance the head of technology knew that he had an issue with the skills of his less-talented programmers, but at least he had those programmers on staff to keep up with the mountain of work his department was responsible for.

I asked this manager why he had not addressed the issue of his poor performers. "Firing them would be very disruptive," he told me. "Most of the time they're good enough. It's just easier to keep them."

When there is a need to do something and Reluctance to Change is the reason for the delay, sometimes a crisis is needed to force the issue. Firing people is never pleasant, but it is necessary when people cannot do their job—and even more necessary when their work creates more work for others on your team.

BARING THE BARRIER

You know the old saying, "The more things change, the more things remain the same"? I think the real truth of that statement is "The more change is needed, the more things remain the same." People don't want to change because they are happy the way they are; they are comfortable doing what they are doing. The effect of change is unknown. Not knowing what your work will be like going forward (or whether you can do it) can be very stressful; people want to avoid stress and find their own comfort zone. When they become confident and experienced in an existing process, they don't want to change.

Reluctance to Change is classic *human* behavior, not just *business* behavior. It is one of the easiest barriers to uncover (in some cases, the required changes are well known and blindingly obvious) but one of the hardest to break. Everyone in the organization—from an employee with the least amount of responsibility and the least ability to influence anything, to the person with the most responsibility—is susceptible to this emotional response. While the Avoiding Controversy barrier also has a very human element to it—people avoid the pain of confronting others—the Reluctance to Change barrier is very much about a person dealing with his or her own emotions; people are afraid of change.

As a result, lots of ideas within the organization about what the company can do to improve itself are ignored. And it leaves a lot of opportunity for change.

BREAKING THE BARRIER

As we pointed out with the computer programmers, sometimes a crisis forces change—or forces people to acknowledge that change is needed. But changing in response to a crisis has its own inherent problems. It is far better when change is carefully planned and there is no pressure to hit a deadline.

Just like the Avoiding Controversy barrier, Reluctance to Change is a behavioral barrier. And justs as we saw in chapter 1, a deliberate, considered process will also help identify where there is Reluctance to Change and will help that change take place. The introduction of a good change process is the first step in breaking this barrier because it lets managers know that change is important and expected. It is the first step in making employees realize that they cannot continue to operate the same way when there is a less complex, less costly, more effective way of doing so.

Second, a formal change process exposes publicly where people are Reluctant to Change. It forces managers to examine and defend the reasons that change has not occurred.

In the case of the electricity company linemen, there was no pressing reason to do things differently. (This is a classic case of good being the enemy of great.) Here a good change process provided the impetus to get better, and the idea that had been dismissed earlier was surfaced again and acted on. It is very difficult to track the precise cause of outages—they depend on storm frequency and severity as well as other factors—but some two years after the idea was implemented, it was reported that 15 percent fewer outages were caused by trees damaging power lines.

When the retail company went to the wireless phone carrier as a backup, again the process provided the impetus for change. One of the hardwire lines was replaced by a wireless carrier as a backup. In the second year of the change, there were *no* reports from any store of both systems going down at the same time, and all the data was transmitted successfully every day. This allowed far better real-time decisions to be made by headquarters and transmitted back to the stores.

With the programmers, the manager's Reluctance to Change resulted in highly visible problems. You might think that two crippling website outages would have created sufficient urgency to spur change, but that was not the case. Change came about because the process exposed the reasons for the Reluctance to Change. The bottom 5 percent of programmers were let go. It may be coincidental, but the bank has not had a website disaster in the ten years since the programmers' skills were upgraded. The head of technology later admitted to me that he would not have addressed the issue had he not been forced to.

But the real way to break this barrier is not merely by instituting a change process that will expose it and the ideas that have been blocked because of it. The lasting solution is through culture change. And that takes management effort. We will explore how to drive culture change in more detail in chapters 9 and 12, but it starts with education. Managers need to let employees know that change is expected and that it starts at the top of the organization. The process will expose the Reluctance to Change barrier and implement projects that require change. Once the projects begin to be implemented and the feared adverse consequences fail to materialize, the Reluctance to Change barrier will begin to evaporate and the entire organization will begin to feel more comfortable with change.

The culture change is also driven by praising and rewarding people who come up with brave ideas—and making the ideas happen. "Just try it" should be the mantra. If somebody comes up with a brilliant, creative, thought-provoking idea for change, make a hero of them in front of the whole company.

As the culture change kicks in, people who continue to be reluctant to change will be exposed because they will have to explain their reason for *not* wanting to do something. Because this barrier is so rooted in human behavior, many of the reasons people offer for not changing will seem quite foolish. It is important to remember that the real reason for the reluctance typically is not the stated one but one born out of fear of the unknown. In today's fast-paced world, the ability to change and adapt is critical for survival—for humans as well as companies.

THE BARRIER IN BRIEF

TAKEAWAY: Of all the eight barriers, this is one of the most widespread and damaging. People are creatures of habit, and when there is no urgency to change, they will not. Change is stressful because people do not know how it will affect them.

SOLUTION: A good change process will reveal where the Reluctance to Change barrier exists and will provide a one-time fix by liberating ideas. Sometimes a crisis will provide the impetus to force change to happen. Some barriers are harder to fix than others; there is no easy, long-term solution to this barrier. The real answer comes in creating a culture that expects change to happen.

LOOK AT YOUR ORGANIZATION

What is your organization not dealing with because of a Reluctance to Change? Specifically, what is not being dealt with because:

- It is not broken.
- There is no urgency.

What are *you* not dealing with because of:

- Lack of urgency
- Complacency

CHAPTER 4

BARRIER 4: ORGANIZATIONAL SILOS

RECENTLY I WORKED WITH A CLIENT IN NEBRASKA and after finishing our work for the day in Omaha, Dave (one of the senior executives) and I drove in the fading sunlight to Fremont. I was struck by the beauty of the landscape: cornfields mixed with farmhouses—this has to be one of the most beautiful early-evening drives in America. As the setting sun gave the golden corn a special glow, I noticed the grain silos on the horizon rising into the sky. "They are essential to our existence," said Dave, a Nebraskan native. "We need them to store the grain. They give structure to our communities."

In just the same way, silos are necessary in companies. They provide the structure that allows companies to work. Every company is split into divisions, departments, or groups, such as sales, technology, and finance. This structure allows expertise in different areas. In companies, silos tend to be places where information, focus (another word for choosing priorities), and control flow up and down. But company silos also cause problems—that same structure prevents the flow of information, focus, and control outward. And in order for a company to work efficiently, decisions need to be made across silos. If a bank decides to change its credit approval process, for example, it would likely have to include many different departments—consumer lending, private banking, small business lending, corporate lending, credit, loan review, audit... and perhaps others. In fact, as much as 60 percent of the ideas generated in the processes I have worked with cut across silos. This is because companies find ideas that cross silos particularly hard to implement. In terms of organizational impact, the Organizational Silos barrier is one of the greatest. And any change process has to address this head-on.

Organizational Silos is one of the structural barriers, and it is also a tricky one because silos themselves are a necessary evil. Organizations need the structure silos provide—but that same structure causes nonaligned priorities, prevents the flow of information, and inhibits decision making across the organization.

HOW ORGANIZATIONAL SILOS FORCE COMPANIES TO DO DUMB THINGS

Car insurers will send you a renewal notice a month before your insurance is due to expire, giving you the chance to accept or decline coverage. Thus, if your insurance renews February 1, you will get a notice dated January 1. Typically, your premium will increase if you have had an accident the previous year.

But what happens if you have an accident on January 15—between the time your renewal notice goes out and your renewed policy goes into effect? At one insurer I worked with, if you had an accident during that time, your premium would not increase for 13 months. If information was shared in real time between the claims department (to which people reported accidents) and the sales department (which calculated clients' premiums), the company could "catch" those in-between accidents. A simple (and inexpensive) systems fix would have allowed the increased premium to be collected an entire year earlier.

The first type of problem we see in the Organizational Silos barrier has to do with nonaligned priorities. The change hadn't been made because two silos, sales and technology, had different priorities. Renewal notices were sent out by the sales department. The systems adjustment was the purview of the technology department. To sales, getting the systems changed was a priority—it would mean more revenue for the company. And increased revenue would reflect well on the sales manager. But of course she had little control over how things were prioritized in the technology department.

The technology department viewed this as a low-priority project. After all, it was estimated that the reprogramming would cost about

$20,000—a relatively low sum for a department spending millions of dollars a year. For a department in which importance was measured by the size of the spend, the project just wasn't important enough. So the project wasn't given the same attention as the high-cost initiatives, where the technology folks could show their true value. Small fixes were not as intellectually challenging as complex systems upgrades or adding amenities to products for customers. The top technology people were used on those long-term, highly visible systems upgrades, and the head of technology was not even aware of the sales department's request. In addition, it wasn't clear what the financial benefit of making the change would be to the company.

To sales, this was *the* high priority. The sales manager didn't know how much revenue was being lost, but generating income went to the core of her very existence, and every little bit counted. To technology, it was just one more thing on a long list of projects that were all considered "top priority" by various silo owners. The technology department had to prioritize its projects somehow, and selecting large, visible, and difficult projects as a first priority seemed as natural as deciding that a low-cost fix probably wasn't going to be all that important.

Part of the value proposition for a moving company is ensuring that customers' furniture is not damaged during the moving process. The harm to a company's reputation is just as costly as having to replace damaged items. People don't want to hire a mover with a reputation for breaking things, and moving companies rely heavily on referrals from happy customers for new business. Most moving companies go to great lengths to ensure that damage is kept to a minimum, and they invest heavily in training for their employees. But of course, accidents happen, and when they do, they result in annoyance and frustration for the customer and reputational and monetary damages to the moving company.

One national moving company was self-insured—that is, rather than buying an insurance policy to cover damages to customers' furniture, it paid out itself for its own damages. The company's claims department was trying to keep as low as possible what it paid out in damages. The head of claims pored over the claims and payout data, looking for some insight into how he could reduce claims, but the figures remained steady.

The company cut the data in many different ways to try to get a handle on the claims it was paying out. Was damage related to time of day (were the drivers tired), to geographic location (were some areas not as well managed), or to type of house (was the presence of stairs more likely to cause damage)? During my work there, the company decided to sort its damage data differently. Rather than continuing to look at the data in the traditional way, the company cut the data by the type of item that was being damaged. The results were revealing. More than 25 percent of damage claims—almost $700,000 a year—were for damage to dining room tables.

The results were as surprising as they were revealing. The company managed very successfully to transport glass, antique furniture, artwork, and sensitive electrical equipment, such as computers. Why was it failing so badly with such a traditional, sturdy piece of furniture as a dining room table?

The mystery here resulted from the second aspect of the Organizational Silos barrier—knowledge and information do not flow freely across silos. The drivers knew exactly why dining room tables were being damaged in such great quantity. When the claims department asked them about the high rate of damage to dining room tables, the reason became clear. Typically drivers used the dining room table as a worktable to pack the rest of the home. As a result, it often became scratched. And because the table was being used in the packing process, it was also one of the last items to be loaded onto the truck. If the table was not secured properly, it would be the first item to shift around and get damaged during transit. Or, worse still, if an item actually fell out of the truck when the door was opened, it was inevitably the dining room table.

A food manufacturer was using more than 30 different chocolate flavors across its various products—just about every available flavor of chocolate in the industry. Different chocolate flavors were used in ice creams, cookies, cakes, prepared food mixes—you name it. There were flavors made from single-source cacao beans, each sourced from a different country, and flavors with minuscule variations in the amount of cocoa solids and sugar. Each product manager was convinced that his or her product needed a different chocolate flavor from the other products within the company, and each manager took great pride in the foods that were based on the distinct flavors. Each product and product manager essentially became its own silo.

This meant that the company had to keep inventories of more than 30 different chocolate flavors and had no real purchasing power because it was not buying any one in sufficient quantity. Keeping track of all those different flavors was costly and inefficient; the finance department alone had to deal with many dozens of different ingredient suppliers, process multiple invoices, and cut multiple checks.

Even worse, market research showed it was not necessary to have such a wide variety of chocolate flavors. A costly taste test, made necessary by the fact that all the product managers refused to give up their distinctive flavors, showed that across the products, an average of 80 percent of consumers could not discern any difference between a more expensive chocolate flavor and a cheaper one when used in a product. Why was this lack of coordination happening, and how could it be fixed?

The Organizational Silos barrier also kicks in when managers of each silo want to do things "their way," as in this example. This desire to maintain control is what caused the great chocolate flavor explosion. In such situations, managers often believe that they are acting in the best interests of the company. If they can make their department (or, in this case, candy, cake, or cookie) the best it can be, how can that not help the company?

BARING THE BARRIER

There are three aspects to the Organizational Silos barrier:

- Nonaligned priorities
- Lack of information flow
- Lack of coordinated decision making across silos

Silos occur naturally because of the way organizations are structured. Each part of a company reports up to a manager who has responsibility only for that part of the company. But none of the parts is truly independent. Each relies on others to perform its function, and the company performs well only when each of these sometimes many parts or units work closely together.

> Organizations need the structure silos provide—but that same structure keeps information, focus, and control from flowing across silos.

This kind of company structure is also necessary because it keeps accountability and responsibility in the silo. It also fosters a sense of independence and pride of ownership, which is a good thing. Senior management's role is to look broadly at the organization; a department manager's is to look deeply into his or her own area. The problem is, doing this creates what I call "tower vision." Managers tend to look up and down only within their own silos—never looking around or across—so all they see, and tend to think about, is their own silo. They don't know what is happening elsewhere in the organization or how their actions impact other areas. They act primarily in the interest of their own silo.

This makes sense. After all, when you are a division manager, your priorities naturally and appropriately center on your division. You may not even be thinking about other groups. And when you have to make decisions that may affect other silos, you are conditioned to think about your own silo first.

Just because a course of action makes sense for a silo manager doesn't mean it is the best way to do things or even in the best interests of the entire company. From a company point of view, silos need to work together. But too often that doesn't happen. Problems arise when departments do not share the same priorities, knowledge, or information, and when managers work in an independent, entrepreneurial manner—in short, when people are operating with tower vision.

You see the Organizational Silo barrier at work all the time. Every manager is part of a silo and has been frustrated when his or her priorities did not align with someone else's in a different department. (Can you remember telling a colleague that whatever you needed was *really* important? Or telling another colleague that you were doing something that has a higher priority? We have all been on both sides of the equation.)

Customers also see the Organizational Silo barrier at work. Think about the process of buying a new car. The salesman at the dealership sells you a car but has to rely on a computer system to tell you if it is in stock. The dealership's sales department is run by a sales manager, who has no control over how the computer system works. She relies on another unit to keep technology running smoothly.

The salesman also needs to know how quickly he can get the car to you. This is also not in his manager's control. Even if the auto manufacturer actually has a car in stock in the color and with all the features that you want, and even if the computer inventory program is accurate, it is up to the distribution department, under the control of yet another manager, to get the car to you. And if you want to finance the car, that is yet another department—and another department the salesman and his manager have no control over. It is only when all of these units within the dealership operate successfully together that the salesman is able to make you happy with the purchase of your new car.

The Organizational Silos barrier is in play even when you are doing something as simple as ordering a meal. The teams in the kitchen have to be coordinated to make sure that all parts of your meal come out at the appropriate times and that all the meals for one table are ready together. If the silos do not work together, you end up with one part of your dinner being cold while the other is hot, or someone at your table staring hungrily while the rest of you eat.

BREAKING THE BARRIER

To break the Organizational Silos barrier, the goal is not to destroy silos themselves but to eliminate the problems that silos cause. That is a critical distinction. Managers may be tempted to think that getting rid of silos is the answer. But the structure that silos bring is very important in terms of creating accountability and responsibility within the organization. Silo managers know clearly what they are responsible for. Cooperation, communication, and collaboration are the three keys to working across silos. Those are components that ideally any successful working relationship would have, but they are *must-haves* if you are going to break the Organizational Silos barrier.

You can break this barrier when knowledge, focus, and control are shared among more than one silo. The solution is about losing tower vision and being able to look at—and see—things from a different person's or department's point of view.

Breaking this barrier is also not about proving who is "wrong" and who is "right." It is perfectly understandable why silo heads have different priorities and why they believe that they are doing the best thing for the company when they are doing the best thing for their silo. When managers have been given responsibility and authority, it is only natural that they will choose to exercise them—and not always in moderation. When decisions to reprioritize do get made, it is because collaboration or communication has allowed a shift in perspective.

In the case of nonaligned priorities at the insurance company, the technology department did not do a cost-benefit analysis of every dollar it spent. And the head of sales could not even make a strong case for the change. She had no dollar figure attached to her request—she just had a hunch that the company was leaving a lot of money on the table. Technology had to balance the priorities of all departments. Cost-benefit analysis was important, but it was not the only basis on which a decision was made. Technology departments also base their technology priorities on customer service, ease of systems use, corporate priorities, and in some cases governance requirements.

Understandably, the heads of sales and technology had different priorities. What was needed was a way to evaluate these priorities. A good change process brings to light ideas such as adjusting insurance premiums a year earlier and allows them to be evaluated in a more impartial, balanced fashion. When the two departments—sales and technology—both focused on getting the fix made, their cooperation resulted in more than $1 million a year in increased revenues, at a cost of just $20,000.

With the moving company, information needed to be exchanged across two silos—the claims department and the drivers—that normally would have little if any need to communicate beyond the rather rote process of verifying claims to ensure that the damage was done before payment was made.

The breakthrough here was not merely that the claims department had to look at the information it already had in a different way but in the realization that it needed to get more information from another department—it had to cross the silos. Sorting its own data differently gave the claims department the *what*; talking to the drivers gave it the *why*—and the means to solve the problem.

The solution in the moving company was to provide each truck with a rolled leather cover for dining room tables. The drivers could still use the tables to pack, but now the tables were protected. All trucks were also fitted with a simple harness that (if used correctly) would keep the tables secure in transit. Really solving the problem also involved making sure the workforce would use the table covers and harnesses. This was accomplished through a series of pay-related incentives and disincentives.

Within two years, and at an annual cost of $50,000 in incentive payments, the damage to dining room tables had declined to less than $100,000 a year. The one-time cost of providing table covers and harnesses was more than covered by the first year's savings. The company saved almost $600,000 a year on an ongoing basis, and, of course, reputational risk was dramatically improved.

Interestingly, this situation also showed how even within silos, information needs to be shared. Because the drivers were scattered about the country and worked independently of each other, there were silos within silos. Individual drivers knew what the problem was, but because they did not communicate with each other, there was no recognition of the size or scope of the dining room table problem.

These first two examples of the Organizational Silo at work are caused by purely structural barriers. In the insurance company, the technology department placed too much emphasis on the size and complexity of a project and not enough on the value it would bring to the company. At the moving company, the driver and claims silos were not communicating with each other. The last example of the chocolate flavors is a little more about individual choice and silo owners not wanting to give up control, but it was also allowed to happen because of the structure of the company. Independence across silos often occurs with full knowledge that the behavior is at odds with the rest of the organization—and total disregard for that fact.

Human nature forces people to want to do the best they can within their own "sandbox" at the expense of everybody else. "Owning" a function or a part of a business naturally brings forth a manager's entrepreneurial spirit, and you don't get to be head of a silo without being competitive. Managers rationalize their lack of cooperation as "I've been given this area to run as I see fit and I need to do the best job I possibly can. And if that means that someone else's chocolate flavor isn't good enough for my ice cream filling, I will order my own!"

Clearly, more than 30 chocolate flavors at one company is the entrepreneurial spirit run amuck. Even though you are responsible for your own silo and its performance, you are just one piece of a larger whole. So all silo owners—not just one—have to give up a certain amount of control for the benefit of the entire organization.

This is easier said than done, of course. We are, after all, in typical silo heads talking about a group of very focused, highly competitive individuals. A good process to remove barriers highlights where cooperation is not occurring, and it points out the consequences of those lapses. It puts in place measures to ensure that decisions are not made in isolation going forward.

Armed with the data about consumer preference, in the face of a company-wide mandate to reduce complexity and a challenge for the silos to work together more closely, the number of flavors was reduced to a core group of eight, and the silos themselves created a cross-silo review process for managers if they wanted to deviate from those eight. This example of self-policing broke the Organizational Silos barrier at the food company.

THE BARRIER IN BRIEF

TAKEAWAY: Organizational Silos create a natural barrier that is tricky to break down because the silos themselves are a necessary evil. Organizations need the structure silos provide—but that same structure prevents the flow of information, focus, and control outward.

SOLUTION: Because you cannot do away with silos, you have to devise ways to connect them. As a client recently said about the PGI Promise® process, "Perhaps the most important value the process brings is in turning towers into 'tunnels.'"

> The goal of breaking this barrier is not to smash silos but to "turn towers into tunnels"—to get people to cooperate across silos.

LOOK AT YOUR ORGANIZATION

- What priorities do you or your department have that are not aligned with another's? Put yourself in the place of the other silo. What would make that silo realize that your need was a priority?
- What information do you or your department have that could be useful to others? What information or assistance do you need from another silo that you are not getting?
- In what areas would increased collaboration and giving up some autonomy be more beneficial for the company than maintaining your individuality?

CHAPTER 5

BARRIER 5: MANAGEMENT BLOCKERS

JUST AFTER I LEFT COLLEGE, I HAD THE YOUTHFUL dream of becoming a top British journalist. I was not good enough to get into the best training program—the BBC News Training Program—which took just ten to twelve kids a year. But I did manage to get in the next best, a regional newspaper training program based in a city just north of London.

We produced a regional evening newspaper. The news editor, Bill, was a wonderful old-school journalist who was firm but very fair. He proved a mentor to many young reporters who even today are dispersed throughout the British national press. He also had the ability to make or break reputations—most good stories start with a tip to the news desk and Bill had the power to decide which reporters covered the stories. The aim for the newspaper and its journalists was to discover an excellent story before the national newspapers got hold of it. In that way the reputations of both the journalist and the newspaper were built.

Toward the end of my two-year stint, Bill got a very strange tip about someone's next-door neighbor planning an African coup. As it was so bizarre, it was not the sort of story he would give to his top journalists, so I was assigned to check it out. In those days, Uganda was run by the infamous dictator Idi Amin. It turned out that the neighbor in question was the head strategist for Amin's main rival. This was not just a national story but potentially an international one. I persuaded the tipster to secretly record a conversation with his neighbor, and I took a photographer with me to London to take pictures of the neighbor rendezvousing with a diverse cast of characters. Within a few days, I had a superb story backed up with a tape recording and photos. We were ready to go live.

Bill was excited. He knew what we had, and he took it to his boss, the associate director for news. Half an hour later, Bill told me the paper would not be running the story. The word was that this was not the typical human interest story that a regional daily would cover; instead, it was an international political story not suitable for the paper. My heart sank. This was the best story I had come across in my two years as a journalist, so why did the newspaper spike it? It turned out that the associate director had been trying to kill the training program of which I was part. It would not look good if a rookie from the program came up with such a strong story. The story was not even discussed by members of the editorial board. I had met my first Management Blocker.

There is a happy ending. I sold the story to the London *Sunday Times*, spent two days as a "researcher" working with top professional journalists to flesh it out, and saw it make the front page (August 29, 1982) with my name as the writer. Nevertheless, my romantic dreams of becoming a journalist were tainted with frustration and disillusionment.

I eventually moved on to another field, but this memory stays with me as I work with organizations around the world that face this barrier.

I had learned my first early lesson about the Management Blockers barrier. When someone's way of life is threatened by an idea from another person, he or she resists it. From a purely logical point of view, the resistance to the idea makes no sense, but there are other factors at work. Management Blockers are very different than those managers who display Reluctance to Change (chapter 3). Managers who are reluctant to change often don't see the immediate benefit of an idea. With a Management Blocker, there is a deliberate, defiant act to prevent something good happening for the company.

In every company, ideas, good and bad, get turned down, rejected, or stalled all the time, and for a variety of reasons: lack of time and resources, and difficulty of execution across the company are just a few. This is simply day-to-day management. But when good ideas get shot down for reasons that have nothing to do with the perceived merits of the idea, I call that management blocking.

The Management Blockers barrier arises when managers make decisions based on fear of what their superiors will think about an idea, when they feel threatened and insecure about the person below them who suggested the idea, or when they feel they may lose power because of the idea. It is a particularly difficult barrier to expose because it is a behavior that no one wants to admit to. It is also particularly harmful because often some of the best ideas within an organization fall victim to Management Blockers.

Before we look at this barrier, it is important to recognize that there are good, generous managers who do not block, and not all great ideas get buried. Here is a look at what management blocking is and why it happens.

HOW MANAGEMENT BLOCKERS FORCE COMPANIES TO DO DUMB THINGS

Bank safety deposit boxes can be opened only by using two separate keys: one kept by the bank, the other by the customer renting the safety deposit box. One bank I worked with found that its customers frequently lost their keys. When that happened, the bank charged the customers $10—which just covered its costs to drill the lock and issue a replacement key. Tom, a regional bank employee, had worked in the safety deposit box department for a number of years, and he thought much about the box rental process. Customers who need a safety deposit box for valuable items or important documents probably are not worried about the cost of a replacement key, he reasoned. The cost of replacing a key probably would not figure into the decision to rent a box. And why not make these keys look distinctive, since they are being used for a special purpose? Tom also made the point that having a fancy-looking key for something that was important to people would further justify charging more for a replacement. He wanted to raise the price for a replacement key to $100.

Tom's manager, John, had long been against the idea and had shot it down whenever Tom raised it. John said he was afraid that raising the price significantly would be seen as gouging the customer.

I later found out that John did not, in truth, believe it was a bad idea. He had believed that *his* boss, the division manager, would be against it. John's boss had already been driving home how important customer service was and how much the business should value customers and their views. Customers with safety deposit boxes were usually very wealthy and, thus, were among the very best clients. While John didn't know how his boss would feel, he also didn't want to risk raising an idea that had even the slightest chance of getting shot down.

It is human nature to try to think through what superiors might think about an idea. John thought the idea might reflect poorly on him, and he was afraid that his boss would believe he hadn't been listening to the customer service message. The message Tom and his peers got was "don't scare the customer."

When customers question a charge on their credit card bill, a process called dispute resolution kicks in. The credit card company acts as kind of a broker between the customer and the merchant. The process involves the credit card company sending multiple letters to each party, and problems can take up to six months to resolve. One long-term employee in a particular credit card dispute department had a brilliant idea to streamline the process. His idea was to get both parties—cardholder and merchant—on the phone at the outset to discuss the dispute and see if it could be resolved with just a simple conversation. Not only would this reduce both cost and complexity within the organization, but it would also increase customer service to both parties by resolving disputes far more quickly.

The dispute department manager was against the idea. She said it would be too difficult to get the merchant and the customer on the phone at the same time, because merchants don't work in the evenings when customers are home. The employee believed the merchants would be happy to make calls in the evening if it meant resolving disputes sooner. He believed customer service wasn't a nine-to-five operation, and ultimately the choice was up to the merchant. The rest of the department knew that these arguments, no matter how well founded, would make no difference. Based on previous experiences with this manager, people in the department were not convinced that a concern for the merchant was the real reason this idea was shot down.

In contrast to the previous example in which the manager thought the idea might not fly with his boss, in this case the dispute department manager thought this idea was terrific. And that's why she blocked it. She didn't want to recognize a good idea that someone else had thought of, because she felt threatened by it. Other old-timers on the team knew this because they had seen her shoot down a steady stream of good ideas, to the point that they had stopped offering them. The team also knew that their manager had been described by her peers as someone "who never thinks outside the box."

The manager was all too aware of her reputation as an uncreative thinker; she may also have felt threatened that senior managers might see the person who had the idea for changing the credit card resolution process as a competitor for internal promotions as they became available.

Before an auto insurance company insures your car, the company does a motor vehicle registration (MVR) check with the local Department of Motor Vehicles (DMV) to verify, among other things, your driving record and ownership of the car. There is a cost to doing MVR checks—the DMV charges for the information, and of course there is the cost of employing the people who execute the process.

Car insurance is something people shop around for. So only 30 percent of approved customers actually took out auto insurance with one insurer I worked with, which meant that more than 70 percent of the MVR checks were a waste of time and money.

One employee had a bright idea: "Why don't we do the MVR checks only after someone agrees to accept a policy or renews one?" he asked. "We waste a lot of time doing checks on people whom we never hear from again. And we can make the policy subject to a satisfactory MVR." This seemed like a terrific and obvious idea. But his boss was opposed to the idea from the start and successfully stopped it from being raised outside his department. Why would he be so opposed to it?

The only problem was this simple action would have meant reducing the department's work by some 70 percent, an idea that terrified the department manager. His leverage within the company rested in managing the MVR department, which had a strong say in who was offered insurance and who wasn't. Not only would this idea potentially decimate his department, it would eliminate his power base. Far fewer MVRs would be done, and he would have much less say in who was offered insurance and who was not. His department itself would not be as important to the company. So even though this idea would be a real money saver, the manager blocked it.

The manager kept the idea hidden because he knew that less work meant a smaller department. Employees would lose their jobs, and he feared that a smaller department meant a loss of stature and influence for him.

BARING THE BARRIER

Like the Avoiding Controversy (see chapter 1) and Reluctance to Change (see chapter 3) barriers, the Management Blockers barrier is a behavioral barrier and has its roots in human nature. When people are afraid of looking foolish for bringing up a "bad" idea, when people are threatened by an underling's brilliant suggestions, or when people fear losing power or influence, the impulse is to eliminate the cause. So managers squash or conceal the idea. But the idea isn't the real problem; the real problem is the manager's own insecurity.

My team and I encourage people not to be afraid to fail—occasionally. People should have a healthy respect for failure rather than an irrational fear of it. But this does not mean we are encouraging people to be reckless.

Because anyone with any degree of authority has the power to be a Management Blocker, this barrier is seen at every level of an organization, making it very common. And because this barrier is about preventing ideas from surfacing, companies have no clue about all the valuable ideas that have been summarily rejected, let alone why, making this barrier especially damaging.

It also is easy for Management Blockers to block because in most organizations it's very easy for an individual to "just say no."

Having committees make decisions rather than managers doesn't help break this barrier, because there are other human dynamics associated with committees. It only takes one person on a committee to shoot down an idea (a blocker) for the idea not to progress. In a group environment, there usually has to be unanimity for an idea to proceed. In a committee, people sometimes kill an idea simply as a way to show power. And once an idea has been turned down by a committee, it is extraordinarily difficult to get it revisited and implemented. This committee dynamic is the reason why, when I am selling our process, I like to meet executives individually rather than address a committee, even though doing one-on-one meetings takes more of my time.

It is also difficult to get a second hearing outside a committee for ideas that have been unfairly rejected. You cannot go to your boss's boss without appearing to be going around him or her. You cannot debate an idea that has already been rejected without annoying your boss and getting a reputation for being difficult to manage. For these reasons, most people abandon their ideas and feel frustrated, thinking, "If you don't want my ideas, fine. I'll keep them to myself." If this happens too often, they get demoralized enough to stop thinking creatively and certainly to stop making suggestions.

Of all the barriers, this is the one that generates the most enthusiasm among employees when it is finally broken. As I go into an organization, the workforce typically feels "liberated"; someone is finally listening to their great ideas for change.

BLOCKING IS NOT THE SAME AS MANAGING

Before we take a closer look at some of the reasons why managers block ideas, I want to reemphasize that rejecting an idea is not the same as blocking it. Management is about making decisions. Good managers have to turn down ideas, but they do so objectively, based on an idea's merits and the impact it could have on the broader organization. Saying no to ideas doesn't turn you into a Management Blocker provided you are judging the ideas objectively. Conversely, saying yes to a bad idea just so you don't appear to be negative or a blocker is poor management.

Also, sometimes ideas that *appear* to be good ones prove not to be so. That does not necessarily mean the idea should not have been approved. Nobody gets it right every time he or she makes a decision. Good managers at all levels understand that about themselves and their employees. Again, the key is to make a decision based on objective facts.

BREAKING THE BARRIER

So why else, other than an objective judgment, would a manager say no to a good idea?

Fear of "not getting it right" with his boss is what drove John to bury the idea of charging more for replacement keys. That fear was baseless, as his boss didn't have a reputation for being a tyrant or for punishing or ridiculing people whose ideas he rejected. It was also cowardly—John didn't want to risk looking bad in front of his boss if his boss didn't like the idea. John was afraid of losing some of his own "capital." His fear of taking a risk was paralyzing him—and ultimately would have jeopardized his own chances for success more than taking an occasional risk would have done. People don't strike out only by swinging at the ball and missing; people can strike out just as frequently by not swinging when they should have.

In a perfect world (or at least at the perfect job), you have a boss who wants you to stand out and progress and will do anything to help that happen. If that is your situation, consider yourself fortunate. All too often, however, the exact opposite is the case, and that is what leads to the second type of blocking. One of the worst abuses of authority is when a manager shoots down an idea because the manager is threatened by someone else's potential success. When a manager won't give someone else the opportunity to shine, he or she is not just being selfish and self-protecting; the manager is hurting the employee and the company. And frankly, the boss is being shortsighted. Managers are judged on the effectiveness of the people they manage, not just on their own actions. A person who lacks creativity would be smart to listen to and to act on creative ideas.

It is extremely difficult for an employee to combat this kind of behavior, because the boss is acting *against* him or her. Employees who try to go around such a boss may raise the ire of an insecure person who may well be vindictive.

The less noble reason for trying to keep a department intact is what can be called empire protection. People often see their power and stature as linked to the number of people they control. If that number decreases, they assume their power and stature will decrease as well. Are you measured in the organization by the number of people that you control, or are you really measured by thought leadership, your ability to influence others, and the smart decisions you have made?

Empire protection is not sustainable. In good organizations, this type of behavior is recognized even without the aid of a formal change process. It becomes apparent when the "emperor" constantly opposes the changes that might affect him or her (and the reasons offered are frequently spurious). And when emperors protect their empires unnecessarily, their organizational credibility quickly disappears.

Just occasionally I see a more noble aspect of the Management Blockers barrier. When managers see the potential for their departments to be cut, they are generally afraid for both their employees' jobs and their own. It is noble to fear the loss of employees' jobs, so compassionate bosses might block ideas that would result in unemployment. On its face, that is an admirable thing to do. But if there are legitimate reasons to downsize a department, those reasons will surface eventually. And if they do so later rather than sooner, bosses who were not proactive might well lose their own credibility in the organization. They will be seen as protecting their own interests rather than the interests of the company.

One final reason for managers becoming blockers is because they want to keep the status quo. Let me reiterate, this is not the same thing as Reluctance to Change (Barrier 3), because the motivation is different. I occasionally see a laziness factor come into play, particularly when people are approaching retirement. That is not to say that all soon-to-be-retired people are lazy or that the laziness factor kicks in only with those folks. But when someone appears to take the easy way out, laziness is often the reason.

WHAT'S BEHIND MANAGEMENT BLOCKERS?

By *Dr. Richard Levak*

When you understand the things that cause humans to feel threatened in their natural lives, it is absolutely predictable that Management Blockers are a hidden barrier to change within an organization. Human beings are motivated to avoid the pain of loss, whether it is the loss of self-esteem, power, money, control, or the love and respect of others. This behavior is part of our self-preservation instinct. In companies, when people feel their interests are in conflict with someone else's—particularly someone below them in stature—this instinct can cause "Management Blocking."

We have seen that denial allows people to act impulsively or selfishly and still feel good about themselves. Yet people are also motivated to gain the respect and admiration of others. Depending on the circumstances and motivations, most people can be selfish, self-interested, and self-protective as well as altruistic, generous, and self-sacrificing. A company needs to understand this dual nature of humanity to find ways to encourage great ideas to surface within the company while minimizing the negative impact of pure self-interest.

Research shows that people are more inclined to act altruistically when they perceive that there is a reward for doing so. The reward does not need to be excessive; public praise and recognition have been shown to be very effective. For example, the manager who promotes a cost-saving process, developed by her staffers, that will reduce her department and perceived power base ought to be rewarded commensurate with the value to the organization and the loss to her. That reward may need only to be a letter of thanks or a public acknowledgment that she acted beyond the call of duty.

Because of the bank manager's concern that a more expensive key would go against the customer service philosophy, he needs extra praise for taking the risk of raising the issue. If he were to put aside his self-protective feelings, he should be acknowledged for that extra effort.

Managers don't always have the bandwidth and the perspective to recognize others' sacrifices and contributions, and companies often don't have the mechanisms in place to offer appropriate rewards. Yet if organizations want to unleash organizational creativity, they need to be mindful of the extra personal cost that some ideas entail and find ways to acknowledge it. The PGI Promise® process outlined in this book takes into consideration these dynamics, encouraging problem solving and acknowledging that some solutions involve taking a personal risk.

PREEMPTING MANAGEMENT BLOCKERS

1. For any given change, anticipate which manager in the organization stands to lose power, prestige, or control and therefore may be motivated to block the effort. The company should identify measures that will address the perceived loss, where possible, or at least recognize the individuals affected and demonstrate its appreciation, particularly when the change involves an individual making a significant sacrifice on behalf of the organization.

2. In advance of introducing change, educate managers on how to anticipate the potential losses they may face and how to deal with them. Warn them that there is a tendency to please a supervisor and to avoid things that could displease or threaten management, but advise them that it is okay to do so.

3. Encourage and reward staff for challenging the status quo through public acknowledgment and reward. To become ingrained in the culture, this acknowledgment needs to be consistent and visible to the whole organization.

4. Reward managers for not being defensive or territorial and for acting in the interest of the company at the expense of their own self-interest. Again, this acknowledgment needs to be consistent and public to be most effective.

5. People will act for the common good if they perceive that others will also act for the common good. Encourage a culture in which examples, particularly of those higher up in the organization, are publicly acknowledged. The more these efforts are shown to be the norm within the organization, the more likely the behavior will be widely adopted.

A good change process will break the Management Blockers barrier in a way that liberates both employees and managers. Employees will finally be able to surface their ideas and see them judged on their merits. And because one rule of a good change process is that there are no inquests, managers are liberated from embarrassment and from having to defend their past decisions.

Like the earlier barriers of Avoiding Controversy and Reluctance to Change, this barrier has much to do with the behavior of managers, and individual employees have little ability to change it. Managers have authority and in blocking ideas, they are using it inappropriately. And like the earlier behavioral barriers, in the short term, a good change process helps companies to ensure that all the ideas buried by Management Blockers can be surfaced and judged objectively and by more than one individual. But the true long-term solution to breaking the barrier is to force a culture change within the organization that discourages Management Blockers' behavior.

During my work with the bank, the idea of the "special key" was raised again, this time by multiple people about who knew about and liked Tom's idea. Two important things came to light. The first was that many customers were careless with their keys because they knew they could call the day before a visit to the bank and have the box opened for them for a mere $10. The second was that the division manager thought the idea was brilliant. The cost of drilling the box and providing a replacement key was immediately raised to $100.

Implementing this idea raised $10,000 in extra revenue for the bank in the first year.

When the idea of "conference calls" came up during work with the credit card company, senior management decided to test it, and it turned out to be extremely effective. In one-third of the cases, the purchaser remembered the charge. In another third, the merchant agreed that the charge was a mistake. That meant that only one-third of disputes needed to go through the complex, costly, and time-consuming resolution process. The idea was implemented as part of their change process.

At the insurance company, the manager of the MVR department plucked up the courage to put forward the idea for reducing the number of MVRs. I truly believe he would not have done so had there not been a company-wide change initiative and had he not seen other managers acting courageously and appropriately. This example also demonstrates something else important. Whenever I work with a company, I ask employees at all levels and in all departments what dumb things the company does that they would do away with. It never ceases to surprise me that employees offer up suggestions that could have a significant impact on their own departments—and even their own jobs. When you ask for help, employees typically are selfless enough to offer it, regardless of the consequences. That's what happened here. Not only was this a good idea, but it also was a particularly courageous one. The process gave the manager the courage to bring the idea to light, and it was approved in an objective manner.

An effective change process also makes Management Blockers ineffective for the duration of the process. Ideas are solicited from everywhere and everyone in the organization. Since all ideas initially are considered good ones, the onus is on the naysayers to defend their arguments not to do something. That is why one of my principles for reversing this behavior and breaking this barrier is this: ideas must be easy to get into the system but hard to get out.

So really breaking the Management Blocker barrier requires two things: a way for the behavior to be exposed in an objective and safe setting, and a change in the kind of behavior and mind-set a company will promote going forward. Breaking the Management Blockers barrier is not so much about changing processes as it is about changing people's minds. (In some cases it may involve changing the people who are in charge!)

Individual managers' behavior must change, but those changes must occur within the context of a culture shift—a change in how things are done at the company. You will recall from the introduction that culture is about the way companies do things. It is about what is expected, tolerated, encouraged, and supported. As I pointed out in chapter 3, the discipline or influence of an outside process usually is required to begin to change a company's culture.

John, the timid midlevel manager, must realize that he needs to embrace a certain degree of risk taking. He needs to understand that it's not only okay to take risks but that someone in his position is *expected* to bring up potential ideas for change even though those ideas could well get shot down. Risk-intolerant companies have to raise their risk tolerance. The culture change will be about stretching comfort zones, letting people know that it's okay to take a risk and it's okay to fail. Companies that make this clear remove one type of Management Blockers barrier.

In the case of the boss who is actually working against you, you really have to hope that the company will embark on a change process. It is the best hope for employees who have been blocked by such bosses because it will allow them to surface their ideas. Of course, it is not uncommon for blockers to try to subvert a process that would root out such behavior, but that same process also will expose their attempt to do so.

The empire protectors need to understand that *influence* is the important word, not *power*. Power is when you have the ability to directly order others to do something. Influence is when you can get things done even if you do not have direct control. You gain influence by the way you behave and the things you say and do that bring you respect. It is not a function of how many people you control within the company. There are many cases of people within an organization who don't have many direct reports but who are extraordinarily well respected. While losing headcount may affect someone's power, it doesn't necessarily affect his or her influence. A good process takes away the abuse of power by making decisions subject to wider scrutiny.

For those managers who are lazy, a good process will expose inactivity, indifference, and unwillingness to do the hard work. When inactivity does appear to be motivated by the desire to go out with a whimper rather than a bang, encouraging people to an early exit may be the best solution for everyone involved.

Remember the perfect world (and the perfect job) we alluded to earlier in which your boss is out only to support, promote, and help you? In the perfect world, a company also realizes that change has to occur on a company-wide level and approaches change in a systemic way. If your company does not take this approach, you face a tough road. Sometimes the best you can do is be what Jim Collins, in "Good to Great" (*Fast Company*, October 2001), calls "your own pocket of greatness," in which you take your "own area of work and influence and...concentrate on moving it from good to great."

> If you believe an idea is strong enough and you don't see it being considered, you may have to have other people generate the idea in a different forum so that it doesn't point directly to you. This is not a case of removing a barrier but going around it. Sometimes that's all you can do.

THE BARRIER IN BRIEF

TAKEAWAY: Good ideas can get shot down not for perceived lack of merit but because a manager feels threatened by them in some way:

- Fear of a boss's reaction
- Fear of underlings shining
- Fear of losing power and influence
- Fear of having to do work

Employees are generally powerless in such situations. When Management Blockers are at work employees feel frustrated, and good ideas never get proper consideration.

SOLUTION: Companies have to ensure that there are processes that allow ideas to be surfaced and considered in an objective way.

LOOK AT YOUR ORGANIZATION

- What ideas have you "blocked"—shot down or kept hidden for reasons that had nothing to do with their merits?
- What ideas of yours have been blocked that you think are worthy of being resurfaced?
- How can you get your ideas introduced by someone else?

CHAPTER 6

BARRIER 6: INCORRECT INFORMATION AND BAD ASSUMPTIONS

NEW YORK CITY TAXI DRIVERS HAVE A REPUTATION— largely undeserved in my experience—for being surly and difficult. Some people would even be so unkind as to suggest that one qualification to be a cab driver is the inability to drive. I even know residents who avoid driving in the city because they are intimidated by the cabbies' aggressiveness. But I love taking city cabs and have never had a problem—with one small exception. One day I visited the chief operating officer of a New York City-based insurance company for an introductory meeting. For such a meeting, I always put a couple of business cards in the top pocket of my jacket so they are easily accessible. The COO and I exchanged cards at the start of this meeting, and we got along very well, so I knew we would meet again.

The meeting ran way over the allotted time (always a good sign), so I was in a rush to get to my next appointment. I went outside and hailed a cab. But on the way to the meeting, my yellow cab was sideswiped by another car. I felt bad for my taxi driver because it wasn't his fault. I told him he could use me as a witness but as I was running late for my next appointment, I couldn't wait around for the police to show up. I fished the spare card out of my pocket and told him to contact me. I never heard from him, so I figured it had all been resolved.

About a month later I went for my second meeting with the COO. We talked about barriers, and when we got to the Incorrect Information and Bad Assumptions barrier, he said, "I understand how this can be a problem in the company. Incorrect information is a problem everywhere. For the last month I have been getting calls from a cab driver who claims I was in his cab when he had an accident. He is so insistent; he even tells me I gave him my card." With much embarrassment, I quickly explained to the COO how this must have happened. But I had no way to contact the poor cab driver, and I have often hoped that everything worked out for him.

In every company I work with, I find that numerous actions are either wrongly decided or not taken because of the Incorrect Information and Bad Assumptions barrier. There are a number of reasons for this. Decision makers may be flooded with too much information and have difficulty sorting and prioritizing it. They may not seek relevant information or they may not be aware of its existence. Information may be just too difficult to gather, or there just may not be the time to gather all the facts and complete a full analysis before a decision has to be taken. On other occasions, managers do not use information even when it is available. That leads to decisions being taken without the correct information. Sometimes managers simply manage with what they have and make decisions based on assumptions, not facts. This can also be a particular management style. The managers may have experienced a similar situation before, or they may just believe they are sure of the right answer. But when those assumptions are bad, wrong decisions are made. In this chapter, we take a look at what can happen when these situations occur. A good change process captures ideas that have been missed because of Incorrect Information and Bad Assumptions, but it goes further than that. All decisions in the process itself are taken using fact-based analysis.

HOW INCORRECT INFORMATION AND BAD ASSUMPTIONS FORCES COMPANIES TO DO DUMB THINGS

You may recall the story I told in the introduction about the medical services company that wanted to reduce the number of HIV tests it was performing on behalf of life insurance applicants. The idea was to pool blood samples from 20 patients. If the combined sample proved positive for HIV, at least one person in that pool of 20 was infected. If the sample tested negative, all 20 people were negative. It was a brilliant idea. But you will also recall that the lab worker had had this idea seven years earlier, and it still had not been implemented. Why was that? It was the Incorrect Information and Bad Assumptions barrier at work.

"The insurance companies will never go for mixing blood like that," one supervisor had argued when the idea was brought up the first time. "Everyone is too freaked out about HIV, so it's too risky." Another manager added to the reasons not to implement the idea: "Even if they did agree to it, we would have to collect more blood from everyone than we now do in case we had to test them again. And we can't keep blood samples long enough for the results of the test to come back." When people started worrying about the insurance company concerns and the costs and difficulties involved in taking and storing more blood, the idea didn't go any further.

Financial institutions retain much of the data they use that relates to their customers. Some is retained for legal and compliance reasons; other data is kept because it could be useful in marketing additional products to customers. And it costs money to store data. Although data storage costs are going down on a unit cost basis, one bank I worked with saw its costs increase because it was storing more and more data. When I started working with the company, it had seven data centers, and the amount of data being kept grew 6 percent in just the four months I was there. None of the data had to do with the project—this was simply the natural growth rate of data storage in the company.

Some of the increase was related to company growth, but that didn't come close to explaining all of it. Data storage costs were spiraling fast enough to cause concern and appeared to be out of control.

The manager of the data centers didn't have detailed information on the data being stored. He ordered some research into the type of information being kept and whether it was ever used after storage. When the research revealed that email traffic was a big component of the stored data, the manager asked himself whether all the emails that the bank sent or received had to be stored. The problem lay in determining which emails might be needed later. You don't know what you need until someone asks for it, so it's almost impossible to say which emails would have to be kept. Still, he figured that there had to be some way to reduce the amount of email being stored.

The next day, as he was using his BlackBerry and scrolling through a seemingly endless email chain to find what he needed, he experienced a real "eureka" moment. "What if we delete the disclaimers?" he wondered. Did the bank really need to retain that long paragraph that describes what you should do if you receive the email in error? Every reply to an email contained all the previous emails in the chain, and the disclaimer was repeated on each and every email. He didn't know how much of the stored data disclaimers accounted for, but some quick research by his team showed that the bank could save at least the equivalent of an entire data center by deleting them.

Once he had this information, he took it to a friend in the legal department. "No way can we cut the disclaimers," his friend told him. Wise in the ways of a good change process, the data manager persisted. "Are you sure?" he asked.

In this case, the company had Incorrect Information to make the decision (how much storage space the disclaimer was using), and the lawyer initially made a Bad Assumption (that the disclaimer had to be kept for legal reasons). There was a substantial cost to storing unnecessary information. When the change process broke the Incorrect Information and Bad Assumptions barrier, the savings in the data storage area were huge. Information overload not only makes it difficult for people to sort through data to find the right material to make a decision, but it can also prove very expensive in its own right.

A grocery store chain was experiencing high turnover among its cashiers. Given that running a cash register is relatively low-skilled and low-paying work, the high turnover was not all that surprising and is common in this industry. The real problem was in how much difficulty the company had in quickly finding suitable replacements. More than 50 percent of the people who showed up for interviews turned out to be unsuitable for the job. As a result, store managers were spending too much of their time interviewing people and not enough time on their other tasks, and stores were not staffed properly, as the vacancies could not be filled quickly enough. Managers found themselves paying overtime to the good employees and, in a pinch, taking stints behind the cash register themselves.

"How hard can it be to find people to run a cash register, especially given how high unemployment is?" one executive griped. Some research done by the human resources department showed that almost all of the candidates who were deemed unsuitable were disqualified because of the answers they gave to some basic interview questions: "How many times were you late for your job in the last six months?" "How many jobs have you had in the last three years?" "Have you ever been arrested?" and "How good are you at serving customers?" The challenge for the grocery chain was weeding out the unsuitable applicants in a more efficient way.

"Why don't we prescreen candidates on the phone?" one store manager suggested. If HR did that function centrally, it would free up the store manager for other managerial tasks. "People will never tell you the truth over the phone," the head of HR answered. "It's a lot harder to lie in person."

As a result, the telephone interview technique was not implemented. Here, based on an assumption by the head of HR, the company retained its costly practice of interviewing candidates in person.

The revenue structure at a payroll processing company was unusual. It charged its clients two separate fees: one based on the number of paychecks it processed for the client company and a flat fee based on the client company's size. Servicing larger clients was more complex, so the fixed fee was bigger for a client with 500 employees than it was for a client with fewer than one hundred. The company began to see pressure on its profits as its costs grew but revenues failed to keep pace with inflation. The chief executive officer wondered what he could do to raise more revenue and instructed all his revenue managers to think about what they might change. It quickly became apparent that the company was missing out on $3 million in annual revenue.

The payroll processing company had many very successful customers. As they became more and more successful, they grew in size. The payroll company should have benefited as more employees went on the payroll, but as companies added employees and crossed each of the size thresholds for the fixed fee, the payroll company failed to increase the flat fee.

Even though the payroll company had perfect information about the size of each company it served (after all, it knew the total number of employees from doing the payroll each week), it did not use the information it had, so it charged its customers based on old, Incorrect Information. It seemed there was no real reason for this other than the lack of impetus to actually make a change.

BARING THE BARRIER

The Incorrect Information and Bad Assumptions barrier should, in theory, be an easy one to break—after all, decisions are either made based on fact or they are not. But too often, managers are prepared to make decisions without the facts or based on assumptions and this can be a dangerous practice. As we have seen, it can lead to wrong decisions being made or excellent ideas being left on the table.

Let's deal with information first. How in this information age can managers overlook or ignore or receive Incorrect Information?

In some cases, the relevant information may not exist. As we saw in the case of the recipe library, companies often rely on employee memory rather than having any formal method of keeping, storing, or organizing data.

Even if information does exist within a company, other problems ensue. Overload can play a major role. The information that a manager needs to make a decision may exist, but it may also be hard to find, lost in the sea of excess. It isn't always easy to tell what information is relevant, especially when people are sorting through a mountain of data. Some companies demonstrate this with a culture of "PowerPoint paralysis." That is, the only way of communicating information is by multiple-page PowerPoint presentations that include so much redundant data that it is difficult for managers to discern the intended message.

Additionally, collecting data can be a cumbersome process, especially if the request is not clearly defined. Companies may not have a method for locating information so that it is available to most employees. Increasingly, companies are also limiting access to their own information. In an environment where proprietary electronic information can easily walk out of the door to a competitor as employees change jobs, it is prudent for organizations to restrict access to their data.

As a result, in complex organizations, managers and department heads rely on others for the information they need to make decisions. If there is a delay in providing data or if the data doesn't quite address what a manager needs to know, it is easy to see how a decision can be made in the absence of the correct information.

Managers also have to assume that what is being given to them is accurate—that those other departments and people with whom they work are doing their jobs. To do otherwise would show a lack of trust and would result in duplication of effort and repetition of work. When people are at the mercy of others for the information they need, the work they do based on it will be only as timely and accurate as the information they get and the people and processes supplying it. If this problem becomes serious, a department manager can sometimes set up an expensive and duplicative "shadow" organization to collect and manipulate data.

Then there is the problem of the timeliness of the data itself. There is a further degree of complexity around using time-sensitive data. Changes in the marketplace, new regulations, or even amendments to company policy can make information instantly outdated. Any decision made using such data is only as good as the timeliness of the information on which it is based.

As a result of all these factors, making decisions based on the correct information may not be as easy as it first appears to be. Gathering the right data may prove to be a very challenging task.

In the absence of accurate information, managers make assumptions. Ideas or beliefs are accepted as certain without any proof. And this happens frequently within organizations. People may *think* they have proof or at least have enough information to make a

> People at every level in an organization should be expected to back up their assertions with data and facts.

decision, but when they are not relying on facts or backing up their assertions, they are in dangerous territory.

Managers get away with making assumptions for any number of reasons: they are respected and knowledgeable, they have a good track record in the company, they have had experience making the same decision, or they are plugged in to the people in the know. Some managers speak with such a sense of confidence and authority that it would never occur to anyone to question them. And, of course, often it is difficult for people with less power to ask questions of those with more. People assume that having authority goes hand in hand with being knowledgeable.

But you can't make good decisions with bad information.

BREAKING THE BARRIER

There is a good reason that one of the twelve principles for change is that the consideration of ideas must be based on facts and analysis, not opinion. Analysis forces people to go after and get the facts (i.e., the right information) to support decision making. The key to breaking this barrier is maximizing the number of decisions that are based on fact and analysis and consequently minimizing those based on Incorrect Information and Bad Assumptions. It won't always be possible to make a decision based on fact, but the goal is to drive fact-based decision making as deeply into the organization as possible.

Let us look at how the barrier was broken down in each of our examples.

With the medical services company, two things happened: the assumption had to be put to the test, and incorrect, outdated information had to be corrected. The assumption was that insurance companies would object to the proposal to mix the blood samples. The only way to test an assumption like this is to flat-out ask the companies if this were the case. It turned out that the insurance companies were happy about mixing blood, provided that should additional testing be necessary, it was possible to determine which applicant had been exposed to the virus. It was important that the medical services company explained exactly what its new procedures would be and how the integrity of individual samples would be preserved. Armed with this information, the insurance companies had no concerns. Their response shot down the assumption that they would not go for the idea.

The second reason the idea had not been implemented was because it would have necessitated drawing more blood. But the technology for testing blood had improved since the idea had first been proposed, and now only miniscule quantities of blood were needed for testing. Enough blood was already being drawn, so extra blood was no longer needed to do a repeat test. The third reason for denying the idea was that blood could not be stored long enough to conduct a second test. In fact, more than half the medical supply company's local offices already had the refrigeration facilities needed. Because of progress in refrigeration techniques, the cost of equipping the balance of the offices was now much less than it had been. The reason this idea had not been implemented was because of a Bad Assumption (about the insurance companies' requirements) and Incorrect Information (about the inadequate quantity of blood and about the storage of blood).

The story of the email disclaimers has become a favorite for me because it highlights every aspect of the Incorrect Information and Bad Assumptions barrier and it also illustrates how well a change process like the PGI Promise® can work in breaking down barriers. This example demonstrates the cost of having too much information, the cost of having inaccurate information, and the potential danger of operating under bad assumptions even when one has the right information. But it's also about creativity, thoroughness, determination, and not taking no for an answer. You can see how a manager's way of thinking changes when he or she is "trained" by a change process to look for solutions and shows how a simple but creative change can have a huge impact when it is spread across an entire company. The example also shows the power of building consensus.

The technology employee had scrolled through thousands of emails over the years. Why did he suddenly look at the maddeningly long email chain differently now? It was because he had been made aware of a problem and, like everyone else in the company, was charged with looking for solutions. After he had his brain wave, he was able to find out how much data was being stored as a result of the unnecessary disclaimer, and he was able to calculate how much money could be saved.

His brilliant idea was nearly quashed by a false assumption—that all disclaimers had to be kept for legal reasons. But by now, he was involved enough in the change process to know that one person's opinion was not enough to kill an idea. Still, a solution had to be created that gave the legal department peace of mind about the risk of removing the disclaimer. Consensus had to be built among all groups so that everyone could live with the solution. When his friend admitted he just "assumed" that the disclaimers had to be kept, the idea progressed. After reflection, the legal team figured out a safe way to remove disclaimers from much of the email traffic in storage and going forward. The team was reassured by the fact that it could be proven at the source that every email had been transmitted with a disclaimer.

The grocery chain was living with an assumption that seemed perfectly logical and likely would not have been questioned except that it had to examine every aspect of its hiring process: what it was doing and why. Sometimes, when data does not exist, you have to go out and collect it by subjecting your assumption to a test. Eager to reduce the money and effort spent on hiring the lowest-paid employees, the chain experimented with prescreening. The company tested the assumption and collected the data, and its initial findings were strong enough for the company to change its hiring process.

The company had wrongly assumed that the most efficient way of finding out about the suitability of candidates was to interview them in person. It turned out that much of the basic information to determine suitability *could* be gleaned from a five-minute screening telephone call. As a result, the hit rate from expensive and time-consuming in-person interviews increased dramatically, and the company needed to do far fewer interviews.

The payroll processing company is a fascinating case. Unlike the other situations discussed in this chapter, this company was not operating under any poor assumptions or using faulty information. In fact, it had all the data it needed to earn an additional $3 million in annual revenue. The company just did not use it.

This case serves as a cautionary tale about how important it is for companies to take advantage of all the information they have about their customers. In overlooking information or not connecting the dots between important pieces of data, companies are losing huge opportunities.

BARRIER IN BRIEF

TAKEAWAY: The right information to make a decision can be difficult to get because:

- It does not exist.
- There is too much information so it becomes lost.
- Collecting it is difficult, perhaps because access is limited.
- You have to rely on others to provide it, leading to delay or inaccuracy.
- It may not be timely.

When information is too hard to get, it will be ignored or overlooked and as a result assumptions are made. Decisions made using Incorrect Information or Bad Assumptions will always yield poor results.

SOLUTION: Make sure that people are basing their decisions on facts—fact-based information should be a company mantra. Do not accept "I guess" or "I think so."

LOOK AT YOUR ORGANIZATION

INACCURATE INFORMATION

- What decisions are you making that involve information that should be verified or updated?
- What information exists in your company that is not being put to good use?
- Are there decisions you have made without enough information because it was too hard to get updated or accurate information?

BAD ASSUMPTIONS

- What decisions do you make based on assumptions rather than facts?
- What decisions get made in your company based on assumptions rather than facts?
- What assumptions could you put to a test?

CHAPTER 7

BARRIER 7: SIZE MATTERS

WHEN I WAS A BOY, SPORTS WERE MY PASSION, and I'm pleased that all of my kids share my love. In our house, soccer is the primary sport. My daughter's soccer team was selling energy-efficient light bulbs to raise money to subsidize its travel expenses. The girls sold diligently over the course of two weeks, taking orders throughout our town, outside the local shopping mall, and at the games themselves.

Everyone needs light bulbs, but some people need a lot more than others, so the size of the orders ranged from single packs of two bulbs to boxes with 12 two-bulb packs. There were even a few really big orders of 24 or more packs. (I assume these supersize orders had less to do with people's energy needs and more to do with our wonderful local community, which is always ready to contribute to a good cause.) The girls' hard work paid off, and they were thrilled when the team exceeded its sales target by 40 percent. The more money the girls raised, the more they could subsidize the long-distance tournaments they would travel to. However, their celebration ended when the light bulbs came and the reality sank in that the girls would have to deliver all the bulbs to people's homes, which they had promised to do. Because of the size of the boxes, the girls had to deliver in pairs, so the delivery workforce was basically cut in half. Plus, they were expending the same amount of time and effort in visiting houses to deliver the smallest order as they were in delivering the largest, making this task more time-consuming than anticipated.

When my overwhelmed daughter enlisted the help of my wife and me, we were of course happy to lend a hand, but I also used it as an opportunity to teach her an early lesson about the importance of size in a business proposition. "Perhaps next year you could tell people that only orders of a certain size will be delivered to their homes; the others will have to be picked up from a store in town or at the soccer games," I suggested.

"Dad, part of what we promised was that we would deliver these ourselves," my daughter maintained.

I pointed out that people were likely buying the light bulbs to support a worthwhile community endeavor, not because of the promise of home delivery, and that the time the girls spent delivering light bulbs probably would be better spent practicing. (I was pleased that I also managed to work in a lesson about Barrier 2: Poor Use of Time.) She grudgingly agreed that maybe I had a point.

I consider grudging acknowledgment from a teenager a huge victory, even though we had only talked about one aspect of the Size Matters barrier. Here, it was about "overservicing the small customer"—those people with small orders. Size Matters is a structural barrier, and it plays out in many ways: many companies avoid differentiating between customers of various sizes, they don't assess the cost-benefit of small transactions, and they just don't "do the math" on what addressing size could mean either in increased revenue or reduced expenses. When size is ignored in any way, opportunity is overlooked. Size Matters.

HOW THE SIZE MATTERS BARRIER FORCES COMPANIES TO DO DUMB THINGS

In the business world, an insurance broker is critical to making sure that every risk in an organization is identified and covered by insurance. The broker gets multiple quotes for insurance and helps the client company select the best one. In the event of an incident, the broker helps the company prepare and make a claim and manages that claim for the company until it is paid. Fees typically are based on the amount of insurance underwritten. Insurance is a service business built on close interpersonal relationships and customer service.

One particular company I worked with prided itself on its customer service, which it believed was the best in the industry. Training for new employees was extensive, and the company invested heavily in making sure its employees treated all customers exceptionally well. Because excellent customer service was part of the company's culture, this insurance broker found it hard to treat one customer differently than another, regardless of their importance to the company, the size of their claim in question, or the revenues the customer brought in.

Deep down, the broker suspected that the extra service to smaller customers had to be less profitable, but it didn't know how much so. When the change project team finally did an analysis of customer profitability, the insurance broker found that as many as 20 percent of customers were unprofitable based on comparing the amount they paid to what it cost to service them.

Management realized it had a serious problem. It could not ignore the fact that the broker was losing money on its smaller customers, but it also recognized why this was happening, which went to the core of the company's philosophy, values, and training.

When a credit card company analyzed its disputes area, it found that almost 30 percent of disputes involved transactions less than $25 in size. We have already seen that when an item goes into dispute, a long and complicated process, dictated by law, must be followed that involves collecting and sending out information. The card company found that the average cost of carrying out an investigation was more than $25. Every dispute under $25 that it resolved cost the company money.

Suggestions about streamlining the process all proved impractical, as the dispute process is subject to federal regulation. The company was stymied as to how it could stop losing money on these small-sized claims without violating any regulations.

Size really mattered here, too. In this case, transaction sizes were too small and unprofitable to provide the level of service that was being given, but the company was constrained by both federal regulation and its desire to have a fair process for resolving claims disputes.

Food manufacturing companies often use agents or "middlemen" to sell certain types of stock, particularly discontinued items or surplus goods that must be sold before their sell-by date. These items have to be sold carefully; they cannot be sold through the same outlets to which the company sells its regular stock.

Agents often ask for a sample of the product they need to sell, and these products are typically packed in cases. Canned food, for example, often comes 24 cans to a case. At one food company, every time the agent needed a sample, he or she would be given an entire case of the product.

In talking to some of the agents, the company learned that they rarely needed full cases; one or two individual samples were enough to satisfy both them and their contacts. Supplying full cases rather than the requested individual samples was inefficient and costly.

The cost of giving away samples to the agents ran at more than $600,000 a year. This was considered a necessary cost of doing business, and the alternative was to throw the extra stock away, so not much value was placed on full cases of these surplus goods.

Sometimes it is very difficult to calculate the size of an opportunity even though Size Matters. We already looked at how size can matter to insurance brokers, whose job it is to help organizations decide which insurance companies to do business with. It stands to reason that insurance companies themselves are more profitable the less they pay out in claims. They want to be fair to customers during their time of need, but they also don't want to pay more than they have to. Calculating a "fair" payment is not always easy. Claims for property are usually paid based on market value. But what is market value? If you total your car, for instance, what is its market value? It is certainly not worth what you paid for it. But the Kelley Blue Book price may not be accurate. And other factors must be weighed. What if your car had low mileage but more than its fair share of dents and scratches? What if you had just put new tires on the car? Its market value is open to negotiation.

Industry research indicates that the more quickly a claim is settled, the lower the amount an insurer will have to pay out. This fact suggests that the goal ought to be to get clients to agree to a sum quickly, but of course clients will balk if they feel they are not getting a fair settlement and may even choose to engage in litigation. One insurance company decided to increase the dol-

lar amount of its early offers to customers in the hope that they would settle quickly.

How could the company calculate the savings it would realize on each claim it settled early? The company, of course, knew what it was paying once an offer was accepted, but how could it possibly calculate what it would have paid a month down the line, after several weeks of back-and-forth with the claimant? At best, the calculation is theoretical.

In this example, it was very hard for employees to calculate the size of the savings and therefore to justify the increased offers made to ensure early settlement of claims. But difficulty in calculating the size does not mean that the opportunity should be ignored, and it should not prevent a company from pursuing it.

BARING THE BARRIER

The Size Matters barrier arises when the workforce disregards the potential impact of size. There are various reasons companies don't realize the economics of size:

- There has been no motivation or impetus to think about size.
- The company culture encourages employees to treat all customers equally.
- No one has done the math to realize the size of the problem.
- The calculations of opportunity size are hard to do.

The barrier tends to result in three basic types of opportunities:

1. The small-customer issue, as was the case with the insurance broker. This problem is aggravated when customized work is done for less profitable customers.
2. The small-transaction-size issue.
3. The opportunity-size issue, where either the math has not been done or it is difficult or impossible to calculate the size of the benefits of a potential change.

Often employees have not been encouraged to think about how they ought to manage from the perspective of size. Workers at the insurance broker that prided itself on excellent customer service thought about what they did in a *qualitative*, not a quantitative, manner. They were concerned with how well they treated their clients. In a relationship-oriented business, that makes sense.

Overservicing customers is one of the most common problems that occur when size is ignored. I see examples of this barrier in almost all the companies I work with. For example, every bank has a private banking group, which typically offers special services to its largest and most profitable customers. But every group always contains various customers who are not very profitable and don't belong there. The group may serve these customers for many reasons: "They are a prospect and one day will grow into it," "They have another (business) relationship with the bank somewhere else," or "Another family member is wealthy, so the group should serve them, too." But each of these customers is receiving a level of service for which he or she is not paying.

Continuing to perform transactions that aren't cost-effective has the same effect as overservicing clients. But it is hard for companies and businesses to stop doing something when that activity goes to the core of their mission. They are focused on fulfilling that mission rather than on thinking about whether doing so is cost-effective.

A credit card company is accustomed to making money from its transactions. It is hard to shift the mind-set to accepting that it is losing money on some transactions; the belief is that this is just a cost of doing business.

Difficulty in shifting focus should not be viewed as "Reluctance to Change." That barrier is specifically about people not wanting to change because of habit, fear, or comfort. This barrier kicks in when managers don't recognize that there is a size problem.

It may seem obvious, for example, that giving out fewer samples would save the food manufacturing company money, but breaking out cases would be a nuisance and would leave partial cases in the warehouse. Inventory was not counted in partial cases, so accounting for it would have been difficult.

It is surprising to companies when they realize that they are overlooking obvious opportunities. And those same companies are also surprised by the impact that even seemingly small changes can have. Many CEOs have admitted that they are more than a little embarrassed by overlooking what in retrospect seemed so obvious. But it is not surprising to me. These "dumb" actions are not really dumb. They are caused by the hidden barriers at work.

There is a lot of opportunity for creativity when size is considered. One of my favorite stories of this type has to do with what happens every time you or I write a check. When a bank receives a check that you write against your account, it can keep the funds for a set period of time before paying them out to the party to whom the check was written. The bank earns interest on the money it keeps. In the banking world, this is known as "float." The amount of time a bank is allowed to hold the check is strictly governed by regulation, but an employee at one bank saw opportunity. "Why don't we change the order in which incoming checks are processed so that the large ones are processed first? This maximizes the amount of time we have the funds and increases the size of the float." The bank decided to experiment; any checks larger than $10,000 got special handling.

Even though checks of that size represented a small percentage of all checks written, processing them more quickly meant that the bank was able to increase its float by several million dollars a year. This was such a good idea that most of the industry immediately adopted the practice.

BREAKING THE BARRIER

In theory, the Size Matters barrier should be one of the easiest to break because often managers are not even aware of the issue. Merely getting a company and its employees to consider how Size Matters is a huge first step. But that's only a start; in practice it can actually be one of the most difficult barriers to break because it typically requires employees to change the way they serve customers.

Though overservicing an unprofitable customer is one of the most common issues I see, it is hard to fix. The solution is to give up those smaller customers, to charge them more for the service, or to develop simpler products. But how do you tell a customer you don't want his or her business? This goes against the customer service values most companies try to instill in their employees.

The broker found that it actually had the solution in-house. One of its international subsidiaries already had a very successful product for smaller customers that was also very profitable for the company. Claims were resolved quickly and efficiently. The insurance broker copied the streamlined product and offered it company-wide specifically for customers below a certain size. The new process involved standard policies to cover standard risks and used just two insurance companies. There was no customization. Instead of the relationship manager handling claims, they were initially handled by a call center before they were then completed online by the customer, rather than an employee. Claims were handled as successfully as before, but the streamlined process offered much quicker closing and payment time for a claim. The broker even found that companies bigger than the threshold size limit actually wanted to switch to the program because of its results. Size really mattered in this example. The company had been losing money on small, unprofitable customers that were being overserviced; now it could serve them in a lower-cost way that customers actually appreciated.

The broker was fortunate in that it already had a solution in-house. But the head of one bank's private banking group described this problem as "insidious." He recently told me, "This is a battle I have been fighting for the last ten years. No sooner do you think you have cleaned it up than it is back again."

When there is no way to make money or to reduce losses on individual transactions, the solution may be to walk away from that part of the business or to simply stop performing the money-losing actions. With the credit card company, eventually a manager in the disputes area suggested the unthinkable. "Why don't we just forget about the claims under $25?" she wondered. "We can't reduce the money we spend doing each of them, but we can stop doing them." It was a counterintuitive solution for a company that was in the business of making money from its customers, but the solution actually had its own peculiar logic. Safeguards were put in place to ensure that any one customer didn't get more than one credit a month or too many over the course of a year.

There might be reasons that a company deliberately wants to continue doing something unprofitable—to have that service act as a loss leader. But my experience shows that the loss-leader concept is rarely a profitable strategy.

A good change process identifies both problems and opportunities. I ask people to examine every nook and cranny of their business to see what they could do differently in order to increase profits or revenues. This action forces them to consider things that they otherwise wouldn't look at. When I work with companies, I encourage them to revisit past ideas that were not implemented. As you have seen from previous chapters, many good ideas are shot down for the wrong reasons.

In breaking this barrier, it is important to view everything through the prism of size. How much time is being spent on small customers, how much do small transactions cost the organization, how much money should it expect to make, and how much money could it save?

In the food manufacturing company, the solution was to break up cases, which meant that one case could now be used to meet the needs of multiple agents. The company could give away far fewer cases to achieve the same degree of sampling. Agents were still given product samples every time they needed one—they were just given fewer. By breaking open cases and limiting the number of samples, the company saved more than $500,000 a year. Although the cost of the agent samples was easily calculated, no one had previously thought to calculate the size of the opportunity in reducing the amount of free samples. Best of all, the reduction was done in such a way that the agents' needs were still being met. Although the company had to hire someone to manage the open cases, that cost was easily covered by the savings. The financial impact was easy to calculate, but the size of the opportunity really surprised the food company.

I discovered that the salesman who came up with this idea thought of it when he happened to be having lunch with one of the agents. The lunch ran late, so the agent asked if he could drop the salesman back at the office after his next appointment. The salesman watched in astonishment as the agent ripped open the case of food products he had just been given and took in only two items.

The agent came back 30 minutes later, pleased that he had made a deal to sell 1,000 cases of surplus food. The salesman asked, "You had a whole case. Why did you bring in only two items?" The agent shrugged and said, "That's all I needed."

Nobody in their right mind would have dreamed that breaking sample cases would save more than $500,000 a year for the food manufacturer. The company knew how much it was spending on samples; it thought it was a cost of doing business and didn't use the size lens to think of a way to spend less, so it had never calculated the size of the opportunity.

There are two other important points to remember about breaking this barrier. Sometimes things seem so obvious or simple that people get embarrassed that they never thought of it. This happens at every level. I have seen CEOs leave the room when they realized the size of an opportunity that was being ignored, and I have seen junior people squirm because they did not want to bring such an opportunity to the CEO's attention. A good change process should be about moving forward, not about rehashing the past…one of the rules will dictate that there can be no inquests.

> Managers are always surprised at how much money is being left on the table. Make sure employees know that there will be no inquests about why this was happening. Change is about the future, not the past.

Finally, sometimes creativity is needed to get information that will be truly useful in determining the size of the opportunity. With the car insurer, it was impossible to calculate how much money was saved by offering larger settlements up front. But in this case, the company was fortunate in that it could at least calculate some of the savings so that it knew the idea was a good one. Each insurance policy also provided customers loaner cars for up to a maximum of two weeks. The company discovered that reducing the average length of loaner car rental by two days would more than pay for the increased settlement offers it was making. It probably lowered the amount of the settlement, too, but this couldn't be measured. The company based its actions *only* on a small amount of savings that were easy to calculate (though the true savings were likely much more). But the cost and duration of car rentals was information that was both useful and available.

With the Size Matters barrier, not every opportunity is immediately obvious. The approach needs to be this: look at everything, and ask where small sizes cost you money.

THE BARRIER IN BRIEF

TAKEAWAY: The Size Matters barrier shows up in a number of ways. A great challenge for companies is to manage the economies related to smaller (less-profitable) customers. Transaction size also matters, where small transactions result in a loss. Companies also don't think about the potential impact that can result from even simple size-based changes in the way they do things.

SOLUTION: Examine every aspect of your business through a size-based lens.

LOOK AT YOUR ORGANIZATION

- Which customers could be just as well served with a less-expensive product or a different tier of services?
- Are you performing any transactions or services whose costs outweigh any potential benefit?
- Where are you not "doing the math"?

CHAPTER 8

BARRIER 8: EXISTING PROCESSES

I HAVE ALWAYS BEEN EXCITED BY FLYING, SO MUCH SO that when I was a graduate student, I took lessons to become a pilot. I put in enough flying time to pilot small, single-engine planes that could take up to three passengers. To this day, I enjoy the thrill of flying, not as a pilot anymore but on commercial airlines. I am fortunate that my work takes me to different parts of the globe.

I am sure I am not alone in saying that the enjoyment of flying has been lessened by the security process that we all must go through every time we fly. The process is complicated . . . and different at almost every airport. Many things contribute to making it a slow and cumbersome procedure. In some security queues, you take off your shoes; in others, you leave them on. It is the same with your belt. In one location, it goes through the X-ray machine; in another, it stays around your waist. It never ceases to amaze me that commercial pilots also go through the same rigorous security checks. I recently saw a pilot undergoing a secondary search. Of course, there is certainly a need for pilots to prove that they are indeed who they say they are, but once that is established, is there really a need to see if they are carrying weapons or other banned materials? Doesn't a pilot have at his or her fingertips the means to cause untold damage anyway?

It is hardly surprising that the security line is slow and that passengers, confused by the inconsistent rules, get it wrong. And every mistake contributes to a "beep" of the metal detector, which slows the line even further because it indicates that a secondary search has to be done. This slow process happens on one of the few occasions in most people's lives that it is really important to be on time. It contributes greatly to the stress that now accompanies every trip to the airport.

About two years ago on a trip back from London, I decided to spend some time looking at the security process. My kids thought I was crazy and that I ought to be touring the duty-free shops, but I was intrigued. It quickly became clear that there was a systematic problem with the process. The bottleneck that was slowing down the line was not the inspection of the bags, as I might have expected, but the secondary security check that happened every time there was a beep. When someone passed through the metal detector and was tagged as positive, there was a body search. And every time there was a body search, the entire line was held up. All three security lines worked the same way, and all three had long queues of people waiting to be processed.

Two agents were assigned to do the search on each of the three lines—a female agent for female passengers and a male agent for male passengers. Even though this process seems on the surface very fair to all passengers, it was grossly unfair to female passengers, who were being held up unnecessarily. Over the 30 minutes that I watched these three lines, just over 60 percent of the passengers were male and just under 40 percent were female. Because there were more male passengers than female passengers, it stood to reason that more men would be stopped than women. Every time a male passenger was stopped and body searched (which happened frequently), the female agent stood around doing nothing while the female passengers were also doing nothing—just waiting in line to pass through. The male agent did more than 60 percent of the body searches and so worked almost twice as hard as the female agent. There had to be a simple way to improve this process. My mind went to work.

I figured out two ways that the process could be immediately sped up and one longer-term solution that would make it faster still. One simple solution to increase the rate of passenger screening was that if the female agent was idle, to let female passengers go ahead of male passengers. Another solution would be to add a second male agent, so that three people worked the screening process at each line. While allowing women to go ahead of men might seem unfair to the men and having two male agents screen male passengers might look unfair to the women, both solutions would actually help move everyone through the screening process faster. And where would the extra staff come from? From closing the third line. It may seem counterintuitive, but passengers would actually be processed faster if they faced two lines each with three security staff rather than three lines with two staff, because security staff downtime would be less. In this case, a simple process change would be a matter of adapting to circumstances and putting resources where the need is.

On days when there were more female passengers than male, the ratio of screening agents would need to be reversed. The required flexibility in staffing would come from other security tasks; for example, those screening bags can be either male or female and their tasks could be changed depending on the requirements of the security line. Both of these short-term fixes could be carried out immediately without the passengers even knowing it was happening. All the passengers would see would be faster lines.

Of course, the real long-term and most efficient solution would be to have a male line staffed by two male agents and a female line staffed by two female agents. Then the line would stop only if you had two passengers with consecutive beeps, one immediately after the other. You could still operate the third line as a "family" line, with one male agent and one female agent.

Here there was a problem with an Existing Process that the security manager could fix in a few different ways. Very proud of my ideas, I approached the security line to ask for the supervisor. He was smart and very quickly understood the potential, but the problem was how to get the solutions implemented. He had no authority to make changes and was pretty confident that if he suggested the idea, it wouldn't fix the problem as there was no "process to change the process." He suggested I "go online." Then, after much searching, he was able to find a paper form for me to fill in to give back to him. I did fill in the form and I did go online, but I have never heard back from anyone.

Today, a couple of years later, if you visit the same London airport, you will see that lines are shorter than they used to be, but the process is just the same—it has not changed. The problem was "alleviated" by adding more screening lines and more screening agents.

Here, the issue wasn't that the process was broken (everyone knew that); *it was that there was no process in place to fix it.* This is my eighth barrier: when Existing Processes suffer from problems, there is no way to fix them. The truth is, the regular tools that people have at their disposal are inadequate for breaking this barrier at companies. At the airport, the screening process was recognized as a problem, but the screening company did what companies often do to try to go around this barrier—they didn't solve the process problem but they threw extra resources at it, at a much greater cost.

> When Existing Processes are broken, there are no obvious solutions to fix them. There is no "process to fix the process."

In almost every case with the Existing Processes barrier, the idea for change is quite simple—there is little complexity in it. The complexity is in figuring out how to change the process to get the idea done. And this is what causes frustration.

As we will see, a good change process temporarily breaks down this barrier to allow existing processes to accommodate change, but over the long term, this barrier is perhaps the most difficult one to break down. What it needs is a "process to fix processes," and a continuous improvement initiative, put into place after the project is over, is the most likely solution. We will discuss this later in the book.

The example I used above demonstrated a huge flaw in a big process that affects many peoples' lives. And there are similar examples of these types of big process flaws in the companies with which I have worked. But in this chapter I want to demonstrate how widespread and insidious this problem can be within a company, so I am going to focus on smaller, less visible processes, some of the problems they encounter, and how difficult it can be to fix them.

HOW EXISTING PROCESSES FORCE COMPANIES TO DO DUMB THINGS

One telecommunications company discovered that it used in its mailings to its customers no fewer than 84 different types of envelopes. It had envelopes of different sizes, different shapes, different qualities, different colors; some with a transparent window for the address, others without. This meant that the company had to keep 84 different inventories, and it did not have buying power for any envelope in bulk. The company estimated that it was losing hundreds of thousands of dollars a year by keeping such a broad inventory.

One of the senior executives set up an "Envelope Reduction Committee." It had to be one of the strangest committees I had ever come across in any company. And it was also one of the least effective. The committee was promptly ignored by the executive whose brainchild it was once it was set up; no one on it had any actual authority, no one from the senior management team gave it any attention, and while the committee had the stated goal of reducing the number of envelopes, there was no direction about how to do so.

The committee became a kind of internal joke at the company, a view that was shared by the members themselves. "Envelope reduction" became a catchphrase for any initiative that went nowhere. A year later, there were still more than 70 different types of envelopes—and the committee was still meeting biweekly.

It seems like it should have been fairly simple to reduce the number of envelopes from a staggering 84 to a more manageable number—perhaps a dozen or fewer. Unlike the chocolate flavor issue described earlier, where all the product managers were zealous advocates for their particular flavors, in the telecommunications company, although everyone had a point of view, no one truly cared about the type of envelope that was used, so long as the look and the quality represented the company.

But this project was doomed from the start, because even though it seemed like a problem with an obvious solution, there was no obvious or proven way to arrive at that solution. There was no existing process in place to fix the problem. The Envelope Reduction Committee lacked all of the hallmarks of a good change process, in part because the company had no experience with change initiatives. There was no focus or support from management, there was no sense of urgency, there was no ownership, there was no way of building consensus. In fact, the only one of my principles (see chapter 9) that was followed was no up-front targets, which meant that going into the project, there was no targeted number of envelope types that should remain. And this was not a small idea. The potential savings from reduced inventory, reduced suppliers, reduced check cutting and accounting, and increased bargaining power amounted to more than $100,000 per year.

One of the Existing Processes at a credit card company I worked with was for replacement of lost cards. If you lost your credit card a month before your old one expired, the company would send you a replacement that was valid for (you guessed it) just one month. Two weeks later, you would receive a second new card to replace the one that had only just arrived. This was a complete waste of all kinds of resources: plastic, stationery, postage, the human effort involved in getting two cards to you. In fact, whatever amount of resource and effort was used was doubled. And while validating a new card takes only a small amount of a customer's time, it still seems like an unnecessary annoyance for a person to have to do it twice within the space of a couple of weeks. It was the kind of "dumb" thing that had customers shaking their heads and that could help create or reinforce a less-than-favorable image of the company.

Do you recall in the introduction where we said that sometimes the "dumb" things companies do are actually a lot more logical than they seem? Sending out two new cards within a month is an example of that. There was a broken process at the credit card company, and the Existing Processes barrier prevented it from being easily fixed. The credit approval process was on a two-year cycle. So once your credit was approved, the company didn't have to review it again for two years.

Requesting a replacement card from customer service had no impact on that two-year cycle. The replacement card didn't stop a new card from being sent as soon as the two years were up. There were two different processes in the credit and customer service departments, each independent from the other. One process allowed credit approval to be granted, and the other allowed a lost card to be replaced. The credit department did have a process to increase the size of the credit line, but no procedure allowed for credit approval to be brought forward in time. The credit approval process was set in stone by the credit department, and the request to bring it forward would have been very unusual. Most of the time the credit department is asked to extend the time to a customer's next credit review, not bring it forward.

> *Retailers typically need a quantity of coins in each of their stores at the beginning of every day, and these coins are supplied by the bank. One bank used two suppliers of rolled coins for the change it kept in the vault for shipping out to customers. One supplied the coins in paper rolls; the other used plastic rolls. Many retailers, however, prefer paper rolls because they are easier to break at the cash register. But when retailers ordered boxes (one hundred rolls) of coins, the bank's Existing Process did not allow them to specify paper or plastic. What they got was luck of the draw.*
>
>   *Retailers knew, however, that if they ordered a "broken box" (anything less than a full box), they would definitely get paper rolls. This was the only way the bank supplied broken boxes, as it was easier for them to combine the rolls left behind. Once customers figured out how the process worked, the bank began getting huge orders for boxes of 99 rolls. You can imagine the havoc these orders created for the bank. Breaking the boxes created a lot of complication and effort. Now the vault employees had to break many more boxes, store and account for the remainders, and recombine them to form full boxes. These special-sized boxes had to be sorted specifically by customer and loaded in a different way in armored cars. This was happening because there was no other way for customers to be sure they would get just what they wanted.*

The bank's existing process wasn't serving either the bank or its customers well. It didn't take long for the bank's customers to figure a creative way around it. But the solution created havoc for the bank.

> *A health insurer found that it was frequently overpaying doctors for the services they provided to patients. For example, when a doctor performed two or more procedures during the same office visit (e.g., drawing blood and*

performing an electrocardiogram), often both procedures were paid for as if each had been a single visit. This could happen if the visits were coded incorrectly; the error could be caught by looking at the date each service was performed. The insurer also found that it was paying for procedures not covered by the insurance policy, as well as paying claims for uninsured people. This could happen when the claimant's insurance expired or when claimants changed insurance carriers. Sometimes both doctors and patients were reimbursed for the same claim, particularly if each submitted the claim independently.

Every year the insurer did an audit and caught many discrepancies. But it was usually very difficult to recover funds from the doctors because the overpayments were so old and involved the doctors pulling records out of their archives to investigate. Sometimes the amounts paid out to individual patients seemed too small to go after. Given the amount of money the company lost every year in overpayments, it was clear that claims processing and the error-recovery process were both flawed.

Employees in both the claims and the error-recovery departments were very frustrated. They knew what the problems were but had no influence to change Existing Processes to recover overpayments more quickly.

A hospital wrote to patients to tell them how payment for each visit was resolved by their health insurance company and what, as a result, the balance was that they owed. But some balances were incredibly small, and a different letter was sent out for every procedure performed—even if the procedures were done as part of the same office visit or hospital stay. And each letter was three pages long, even for the simplest of visits. The result was that a patient could receive as many as six multiple-page letters on the same day, all mailed in different envelopes.

While the hospital prided itself on keeping customers up-to-date and informed, there was clearly room for reducing the amount of communication that took place. But there was no process for doing so.

BARING THE BARRIER

The Existing Processes barrier may be the most frustrating one for any employee or customer, and it is perhaps the one for which there are the most anecdotes. We have left this barrier for last because it is the one people recognize most easily and the one with which they most identify, as either an employee or a customer.

Over time, Existing Processes have become inadequate (or perhaps never were adequate to begin with) to address the growing demands of the business. In other cases (such as the credit card company), two processes conflict with each other.

Part of the frustration surrounding this barrier is generated because the ideas for improvement are usually blindingly obvious to those who are affected by them—they just cannot figure out how to get them done. Think of my example at the London airport. The solution was obvious, both to me and the local supervisor. How to put it in place was not. With this barrier, there seems to be no way to get from A to B. People know what has to be done; the frustration comes when they can't do anything about it. Whether an idea is large or small, if there is no way to change an Existing Process, any attempts to fix the problem will likely be unsuccessful. How is it possible that 6 intelligent people could not figure out how to reduce the number of envelopes from 84 to far fewer than 70—and cause their efforts to become a company story along the way? Why was it so hard to give excellent bank customers coins in paper rolls instead of plastic? Why would a hospital send out six letters in one day to the same person, when one streamlined mailing would suffice? And why would a credit card company send out a card with an expiration date of just a month and a second one just two weeks later?

In fact, none of the problems posed in this chapter were particularly complex, and in each it was clear what *needed* to happen. Yet none of these seemingly simple solutions could be implemented successfully by the companies involved. In each case, they had either tried but failed or could not even figure out how to attempt to resolve the problem. This then, is the primary characteristic of the Existing Processes barrier. What to do is not complex and is often obvious. How to get it done is not.

BREAKING THE BARRIER

Breaking this barrier is extraordinarily difficult without a good change process. The short-term focus that comes from an initiative such as PGI Promise® removes the Existing Processes barrier, allowing multiple processes to be quickly changed and, as a result, allows literally thousands of ideas to be implemented. Without this focus, frustrations continue and ideas languish.

Let us look at how the Existing Processes barrier was broken down by the change process employed by each of the companies in my examples.

In the case of the envelope explosion at the telecommunications company, the change process provided all the attributes the Existing Process was missing—authority, a goal, a sense of urgency, ownership, and senior management attention. The Envelope Reduction Committee approached its task with a new mandate. The number of envelope types was quickly reduced from 70 to fewer than 20.

At the credit card company, the change process allowed the credit department to see how the inflexible length of credit approval was an issue, and the department, when it was asked, had no problem accelerating the new credit review for anyone who lost a card within six months of expiry.

Their change process allowed a solution to be found for the bank vault's wrapper dilemma. The solution was to add to the ordering process a step that allowed customers to specify exactly which type of coin wrapping they wanted. Although now the bank was delivering two products where before it had delivered only one, all the complexity associated with broken boxes was largely removed. A change was also made so that the default going forward was to deliver coins in paper wrappings rather than plastic.

At the health insurance company, a change in the auditing schedule from once a year to once a month reduced the scope and complexity of the audits. They were now one-twelfth the size and much less difficult to execute. Mistakes were caught earlier and the recovery rate improved because the company was now going after recent claims. Doctors and patients were more inclined to be cooperative the sooner a mistake was identified; it was easier for them to accept they had no right to the money they had been given by mistake.

In some cases, overpayments to doctors were merely deducted from future payments, so doctors did not have the sense that they were surrendering or giving back something. Psychologically, this made the reclaim process a lot easier to bear. Also, the company no longer had to write off claims that were too old or too much trouble to go after.

And finally, at the hospital, its change process provided the vehicle that allowed it to fix its customer statement challenge. The first thing the hospital did was to combine all procedures within a two-week period and include them on one statement. A more complex, longer-term fix involved reducing the amount of repetitive information and redesigning statements to reduce the number of pages sent out. Printing on both sides of the paper accomplished part of the page reduction.

As we mentioned, breaking this barrier is extraordinarily difficult without a good change process that removes the Existing Processes barrier, allows multiple other processes to be improved, and as a result allows literally thousands of ideas to be implemented. But it is hard to make breaking this barrier sustainable. The companies I have worked with typically introduce a process for continuous change straight after I depart, using the framework and the structure that were introduced. Here, the culture is to expect (and be prepared for) change. The small infrastructure of the continuous change program reports directly to the chief executive officer, encouraging new process change ideas to continue to come forward and allowing this barrier to continue to remain broken. Once a successful project has been completed, it is far too easy for the Existing Processes barrier to slip back into place. The program left behind prevents it from doing so.

> You don't realize how difficult it is to change an Existing Process until you discover a problem with it and try to get that problem resolved.

THE BARRIER IN BRIEF

TAKEAWAY: The Existing Processes barrier prevents ideas from being implemented, even if they are simple and well-known and people want to do them. It is caused because there is no process in place to change other processes. The problems to be solved are often not complex; determining how to resolve them without a process to do so, however, is. This causes frustration in customers and employees alike.

SOLUTION: A good change process provides the platform to allow Existing Processes to be changed and simple ideas to be implemented. But this is the toughest barrier to break in a sustainable fashion. A continuous change program, implemented after a change project and run from the chief executive's office, has been shown to work in keeping this barrier at bay.

LOOK AT YOUR ORGANIZATION

- What Existing Processes do you see that are flawed?
- What easy, obvious solutions have you been unable to implement with any degree of success?
- What is really needed to solve the problem? What needs to happen for you to get there?

CHAPTER 9

TWELVE PRINCIPLES FOR BREAKING BARRIERS

OVER THE COURSE OF MORE THAN 20 YEARS HELPING excellent companies avoid dumb things, I've come to realize there are three aspects to such an undertaking: identifying the barriers themselves, the principles that must govern any process to break down the barriers, and, finally, a change process that can lead to sustainable improvements.

In chapters 1 through 8, you've read about each of the barriers. This chapter is an overview of the twelve principles that should be applied to enable change to happen. And in the next four chapters, you'll see how the principles apply to creating lasting change.

Principle 1. The chief executive officer must personally lead and support any change process carried out across the entire organization, and a majority of senior management must also support it.

Early in my career, I came across a CEO who had recognized the barriers within her hospital company and had tried to break them down a year earlier. But she had not wanted to do it herself; she had a very strong and talented management team, and she thought they should run their own project. As she had explained to them, "You're the folks who are going to have to make it work and live with it, so you might as well be the ones to figure out how to make it happen."

The problem was, the CEO's lack of commitment was infectious. Her direct reports quickly delegated the task to their teams. This lack of focus on the part of senior management meant it was impossible to make even a dent in the barriers. The controversial ideas were raised but not resolved. There was no urgency and no clear leadership. Time deadlines slipped or were ignored without consequence. The result was a disaster, and the CEO did not understand why.

If a company is looking for change that encompasses the whole enterprise, the leader of the company *must* lead the barrier-breaking process. This is not to say that the CEO is going to be involved in every meeting and every single decision, and it does not imply a major time commitment on the CEO's part. But the CEO must declare that change is expected, that the change initiative is his or her project, and that it is important to him or her. And the CEO's subsequent words and behavior must demonstrate that commitment.

This principle is important for a very specific reason: it gives the project focus, and without that focus, the project will not work. If the CEO does not take the change project seriously, no one else will. People need to think of the change project as the CEO's own.

At the team or department level, the same principle holds true. If a leader does not embrace the idea of change, there is little impetus for anyone else to do so. Conversely, if the boss says, "This is what I am committed to," it is very hard for people not to fall in line.

Sometimes it is difficult for team leaders to embrace the idea of complete enterprise change. It is the CEO's project, not theirs; it may well impose a different set of priorities and commitments on them and their team, and they simply may not want to change. Strong, savvy team leaders embrace change and use the project as an opportunity to deliver their own agenda for change within the organization. Weaker team leaders resist it.

A good change process is designed to quickly highlight where there is commitment and where there is not, so that any lack of commitment can be addressed early by the CEO and the senior management team.

There are two early tests of CEO and senior leadership commitment. The first is their selection of the "stars" who will guide the project. Will the senior leaders select the very best employees, those who cannot be spared? The same employees who work on all the big initiatives? (These employees are always chosen for good reason. The adage "If you want something done, give it to a busy person" applies here.) Or will the senior leaders chicken out and select the manager who is close to retirement or the one who needs a temporary new assignment?

The second test for senior leaders is how they react when a good friend tries to influence them and uses a personal relationship to try to circumvent their change process. People will likely try this almost immediately. A leader has to make it clear that alliances and politics (and even close friendships) have no currency in a good change process. Decisions need to be made on their own merit.

The test for other less-senior leaders is an early public forum at which they give senior management a first look at their ideas for change. The review is purportedly to preview some of their thoughts, but it is really to determine those managers' own commitment to the project.

Only a few things can prevent a comprehensive change process from working, but failing to follow this principle—the commitment of the CEO and the senior management team—tops the list. In hindsight, it is clear why the hospital company's initiative had failed so badly. It may seem a little rash on my part, but I now tell potential clients that I would prefer *not* to work with them if there is no senior leadership commitment. Every manager in the organization does not have to be in favor of the change process, but supporters need to weigh against detractors. And the CEO needs to be supporter in chief.

Principle 2. The entire organization must be engaged in the change process.

Companies are always surprised at the number of ideas—genuinely good ones—that come from the staff. On average, I find that one idea is submitted for every person within a company. This shows that the knowledge and creativity are there and that employees genuinely want to help make things better.

But there is a statistical truth about all those ideas: around 80 percent of the profit impact of the change typically comes from 20 percent of the ideas. And that 20 percent is usually generated by middle management or the employees who run departments or teams.

You might wonder what the point is of having even the most junior people contribute ideas if those suggestions are not going to have a big impact on the bottom line. There are five critical reasons for involving everyone.

1. Involving the entire employee base provides a huge psychological benefit. Everyone feels invested in the change process and has ownership of it and everyone feels included in designing the new organization. This makes it a lot easier to get the entire company on board when you actually make the changes—people recognize they result from a process in which they have been involved. Additionally, to make the changes stick, it is important to change the culture of an organization. The first step in culture change is to include the whole company in the change process from the start.

2. Involving the whole company demonstrates that there are no "sacred cows." Every part of the organization is expected to contribute to the change. No "special" areas get left out. This sense of equality and fairness is important for getting organizational buy-in for making any changes.

3. Middle management may provide the big-dollar ideas, but small-impact ideas matter. Add them up, and they matter a great deal. These ideas that have smaller financial impact also tend to be the ones that simply help the company run better. A change might be as simple as allowing a call center employee to jump from screen 2 to screen 7 without going through the intermediate screens. Complexity is reduced and customer service is improved only in the depths of the organization, and the people farthest down in the organization are the ones with the best insights on how to do that.

4. Taking the entire organization through a change project at the same time creates a cross-organizational momentum that allows ideas to be considered and quickly resolved by the right people. In short, it introduces a common priority.

5. Just occasionally there is a brilliant idea—a hidden diamond—hiding in the workforce.

Principle 3. The project must be guided by "stars" who are willing to challenge the status quo.

I remember a change project with a hugely successful bank more than 15 years ago. The gold-trading department was run by a veteran who was superb at his job—he was a true industry expert...and a particularly prickly character. He was fair-minded but skeptical. His department was very profitable, so he wanted to know why he should change anything about it. He questioned what I, an outsider, could possibly tell him about his business that he didn't already know. If I had even hinted at the remote possibility that there were barriers in his area, he would have unceremoniously thrown me out.

The CEO took the head of credit out of his job for one hundred days to put him full time on the change project. Making the right credit decisions is the lifeblood of any bank. Removing this person from his daily responsibilities sent a huge message to the organization about the importance of the change project. Although this credit guru knew nothing about gold trading, he and a colleague were paired up with the head of that department to come up with ideas for change.

Using the head of credit as a catalyst for change in the gold-trading department was a brilliant move. The gold trader had complete respect for a fellow professional who was also an expert in his own field. And someone who was smart but didn't know the gold-trading area was able to ask "dumb" questions: "So tell me again why do you do it that way?"

A key principle to breaking down barriers is to use a small team of internal change agents—the "Catalyst Team" in our process—who for one hundred days are pulled full time from their normal role in the company to work solely on the project. Typically these are people who cannot be spared, not those who are looking for their next role. They are deliberately assigned to work in areas they are not from and know nothing about.

This assignment creates an interesting dynamic. Because of their everyday role within the organization, they have the instant credibility that an outsider could never have. But they are also put into a situation where they are expected to ask naive questions. They quickly form an independent view of the area they are working in, and they challenge the leader of that area to consider and come up with ideas for improvement.

In selecting a Catalyst Team, there are four qualities to look for:

1. Intelligence
2. The ability to be a team player
3. A passion for change
4. The ability to get things done

Selecting this team is not an easy task for any company—but breaking barriers is also not easy. It can be pretty straightforward to choose two-thirds of the team; senior management nominates some of the strong performers from their respective areas of the company. But the remaining one-third involves difficult trade-offs. Not all managers can be pulled out of their jobs for one hundred days. Some must be left behind to run the company. But when the right team has been selected, it creates a sense of excitement—the same sort of excitement a sports fan feels at the beginning of a new season when a star athlete joins a favorite team.

The strength of a team like this has also been recognized over time in a different way. After going through the barrier-busting process and the organizational exposure that brings, at least three former team members I have worked with have gone on to be Fortune 750 CEOs in their own right.

So what happened to our prickly gold trader? Working with the head of credit, he and his department together came up with more than one hundred ideas to improve the way business was done in gold trading…and they improved profitability by more than 20 percent!

Principle 4. There must be no up-front targets for the company as a whole or the individual departments within it.

When a company needs to do a better job of meeting its budget or increasing profits, how often have you heard the instruction, "Cut by 10 percent"? In my experience, this is the most frequent way that companies try to improve the way they do things. Sure, this approach means there is some belt tightening that improves the bottom line in the short term, but nothing actually changes. Things are done in exactly the same way, but typically with fewer people. No new ideas have been implemented. And why is 10 percent the right number? Why not 12 percent or 8 percent?

One key principle in removing barriers for change is *not* to set targets. There are four reasons for this, all of which have to do with integrity.

1. The amount of change depends on the good ideas that are released when barriers are removed. Before a project starts, no one has any idea what the amount of change is likely to be.
2. The amount of change differs by area. In a change project, there is no room for a one-size-fits-all approach that comes with setting a target. A target that may be right for one department will be wrong for another.
3. When you give managers a number, that is exactly what you will get out of them—and it is *all* you will get out of them. Some of the opportunity to do things better may well be left on the table.
4. Any change brought about by setting targets rather than changing the way things are done is not sustainable. Within a couple of years, those departments subject to the targets typically return to doing things the same old way.

Of course, managers always ask what the ideal impact from releasing great ideas ought to be. This is understandable. People always want a simple way to measure success or failure. But in breaking barriers, the true measure of success is different. The real question is, "Did you reach your full potential in your department, and did you do it in such a way that work went away or was simplified?" You will never know—or realize—the full potential if you give managers a number to hit.

As part of our change process, the PGI Promise®, managers eventually generate targets to hit, and those targets will be chased and tracked very aggressively. The expectation is that those targets will be 100 percent achieved. But these targets are the *outcome* of the change process, determined by employees themselves and then agreed to with management. And the targets differ by area, depending on the opportunity within each one.

When the time finally comes for setting targets, I encourage people to underpromise and overdeliver. My team and I allow participants to set their own targets slightly conservatively so that they can beat them. We want everyone to be a winner when they come out of our process. Could understating the potential financial impact be interpreted as gaming the system? Perhaps. But this is a small price to pay for creating an environment in which people feel good about beating the targets they themselves established—and understating the potential impact virtually guarantees that the target number will be achieved.

Principle 5. Those who will implement the idea must own the idea.
As I mentioned in the Introduction many years ago, when I was consulting for a big global firm, I would go into an organization, spend months gathering data, determine what the real challenges were, figure out the world's best solution to the problem at hand, commit it to paper in a very compelling way, put it into a "blue book," and proudly present that book to my clients. I had reason to visit one of my former clients ten years after I had delivered my blue book. There it was—on a shelf gathering dust. It was obviously considered important enough to keep but not important enough to read. (He told me he had never even opened it.) The problem with that book was that it was full of *my* ideas. The people whose jobs and departments were going to be affected had no stake or pride of ownership in the ideas. In fact, no matter how great the ideas in the blue book, people were often resentful because they felt like the ideas were being thrust upon them. And they were right about that.

In any change process to break down barriers, the managers who will implement the ideas must own them. They may not do so at the start of the process; in fact, these managers, or their departments, may not even be the source of the ideas. But by the end of the process, they need to not only agree with an idea but also passionately advocate for it. A good change process gives them the chance to become the champion for those ideas.

But what about other good ideas that managers refuse to own? In our change process, such ideas go by the wayside rather than getting green-lighted. I have found that it is very difficult to ask people to implement ideas they do not believe in. If ideas are imposed on them, managers tend to leave those ideas as the very last to be implemented, and you would be amazed at how often an unexpected "problem"—unforeseen at the time the idea was proposed—suddenly arises to stop that implementation from happening. As a result, the idea has a high likelihood of failing.

Because anyone can come up with an idea for change in any part of the organization, an idea may not originate within the department, let alone with the manager or department head. But before the idea is committed to, that manager must be completely on board.

Change comes about when people truly believe in the ideas that they are responsible for implementing. A big reason why the PGI Promise® is successful is that almost all of the ideas come from employees, not consultants. People do not like having ideas forced on them, whether it is by outsiders, their bosses, or their peers. When I do want to insert an idea into a change process, I do it carefully, so that it doesn't seem to be coming from me. And any ideas that I submit are subject to the same rules as all other ideas.

Principle 6. It must be easy to put ideas into the change process but hard to remove them.

How many times have you made a good suggestion only to have it shot down immediately? This can happen for a number of reasons, but, as we learned earlier, it is very easy for a Management Blocker to "just say no." And when ideas can be vetoed so easily, people have little incentive to offer further suggestions.

We have already seen that when your goal is to make sustainable changes, you need to get ideas from every possible source. So, to gather ideas and to avoid them being shot down early, I use the mantra that "every idea is a good idea." That is not to say that every idea will be implemented, but it does mean that each idea will be fully considered.

Any good barrier-breaking process must have an easy way to get ideas into the system. When the change process asks for ideas, the floodgates should open. It is not unusual for employees to generate literally thousands of ideas in a matter of weeks.

But getting an idea on the table is just half the battle; the other half is keeping it there long enough to be fully considered. We know that usually it takes just one person at a group meeting to effectively veto an idea. And revisiting a vetoed idea proves very difficult.

In our process, my team and I change the dynamic. Ideas are not removed from the process even if someone disagrees strongly with them. Dissenters are, however, encouraged to express their views. We ask them to "risk rate" the idea: would implementing the idea be of low, medium, or high risk? Even high-risk ideas remain in the system. The goal is to see if risks associated with implementing an idea can be reduced by amending it slightly.

And we go against another norm of decision making. Instead of someone having to prove why an idea has merit, someone has to prove why it does not. The idea will be implemented unless someone makes a persuasive argument against it. An idea is innocent until proven guilty; the idea is presumed good until proven that it is not. There has to be a credible reason *not* to implement an idea rather than the other way around.

Everyone is encouraged to submit any suggestion for improvement. And because the burden of proof has been shifted, those ideas, no matter how "dumb" they may seem, are hard to remove. Because of this principle and the rules governing the process (such as the lack of inquests), employees feel more comfortable about offering suggestions, asking dumb questions, and thinking creatively. And good creative ideas are hard to dismiss without very good reason. This set of rules is designed to cause a very big, dramatic culture shift in the organization, and one that releases huge opportunity.

Principle 7.   Consideration of ideas must be based on facts and analysis, not opinion.

As well as shifting the burden of proof to the person who *doesn't* want to do something, a good change process also raises the bar for proof. Managers cannot just say, "I think it's a bad idea" or "That will never work." They need to be armed with facts and information, not merely opinions or beliefs, before they can shoot something down. You cannot have your own opinion, but you can have your own facts. For this reason, any strong process encourages debate based on facts, not on people's opinions.

Think back to the case of the HIV testing that we talked about earlier. The department manager didn't *think* insurance companies would want blood to be comingled before testing was done. This was his *opinion*. But when they were asked, the insurance companies did not mind—provided that the test center could determine exactly which individual sample caused the positive result in the comingled sample.

Within an organization, many people like to think they are the voice of the customer when trying to kill ideas. A manager's *opinion* that the "customers will not like that" is frequently heard, but all too often it is just that—an opinion. Do you remember the case of the call center in chapter 1? The head of retail banking did not want to reduce the call center's hours because all of the competing banks had 24-hour service and he believed this round-the-clock service was important to customers. After he actually listened to some early-morning calls, however, he based his decision to limit the hours on fact, not opinion. Whenever a belief or opinion about a course of action can be independently tested, it should be. Opinions are very often proven wrong, and any debate over the merit of an idea should use facts.

Principle 8. Consensus must be built.

Of all of the twelve principles, if there is a "secret sauce" for ensuring 100 percent implementation, then building consensus is it. Any process for breaking down the barriers and generating ideas for change must include a strong consensus-building element. In our change process, participants spend the largest amount of time building consensus—twice the amount of time they spend actually generating ideas for change. The goal of our process is to generate 10,000 or more debates throughout the company...and then resolve them all in one hundred days.

Consensus is built around an idea by upgrading the idea to include the views of all who consider it. This sometimes requires a compromise to the original idea. In a bank, for example, the credit department typically requires corporate lending officers to perform an annual review of each company that it has lent money to so the bank can ascertain that the company is solvent and can continue to repay its loan. More than 95 percent of companies pass the review with flying colors, so the bank's lending officers, who are part of each review, can see them as a huge waste of time.

In one bank I worked with, the lending officers suggested doing reviews every two years rather than annually. They reasoned that cutting the number of reviews in half would give them more time to spend with customers or to make new loans. A compromise worked out with the loan review department was somewhere in the middle. Not all companies should be switched to a two-year cycle; both the lending officers and the credit experts could agree that small loans (perhaps less than $2 million) or loans to companies in a particular industry or with a strong credit rating could be done every two years. In this way, some of the wasted time could be captured. This change allowed the size of the loan review department to be reduced at the same time it created more capacity for growth through increased selling time for the lending officers.

In the consensus-building process, not everyone will agree on everything—and that isn't the goal. But you cannot move forward with any idea until and unless you have consensus among people affected by it.

In my experience, I estimate more than 97 percent of all ideas that companies choose to implement at the end of a change process are determined to be low risk by all who looked at them. They didn't start out that way, but that is how they ended up. Very rarely does an idea get approved without everyone agreeing to it. By making consensus a goal and condition for moving forward, my team and I remove the threat of Management Blockers, we ensure that those implementing the idea believe in it, and we find that the idea is less likely to run into implementation roadblocks.

Principle 9. There must be a focus on increasing revenue, not just reducing expenses.

Figuring out how to do things better is the most obvious way to improve a company's financial performance, but focusing exclusively on costs is a mistake—one companies make time and time again.

You must pay equal attention to opportunities that allow for increasing revenue. Often these ideas will be among the most creative ones from your team—and the ones people get the most excited about. I have found that, on average, 30 percent of the financial impact of any good change project comes from revenue-generating ideas.

There are four types of ideas for generating revenue:

1. *Stop leakage.* Leakage occurs when you give away your services for free or at a discount, even though a price has already been agreed with your customer and the customer expects to pay that price.

A company that supplied simple medical products for home use once described to me its policy of waiving shipping charges for good customers. When ordering supplies, customers would remind the sales executive what good customers they were. Because it was completely within the executive's discretion and control, the shipping charges would be waived. Analysis showed that 85 percent of all shipping charges were waived. No one was tracking the amount of leakage, and authority for waiving shipping charges was not tightly controlled. The company was able to increase product profitability by 20 percent overnight simply by focusing on leakage.

Leakage is particularly prevalent in any industry or company that charges fees for services, but it does not affect just fees. The insurance company that was waiting 13 months to raise the rates of customers who had had road accidents was experiencing leakage.

I find examples to control leakage at every company I work with.

2. *Price for value.* My experience shows that companies are not very good at understanding the true value of the products and the services they deliver to their customers. This is particularly true when there is a premium in delivering the product either very quickly or at a certain time.

An example of this was described in chapter 2 when we saw the importance to customers of being able to send their wire transfers at the end of the day. This area is limited only by creativity. In New York City, the Queens-Midtown tunnel has an express lane that can be used only by taxis and those cars with more than one occupant. But what if, for a $25 toll instead of the regular toll, anyone could use the express lane? If the other lines were too long or an appointment was too important to miss, people would pay the higher toll.

A water home-delivery company (not a client of mine) charges a deposit of up to $10 for a seven-gallon bottle. The deposit is returned when the empty bottle is collected. A busy person can easily forget what day bottles will be collected. For a $5 monthly fee, the water company will notify users the night before a scheduled collection to remind them to put out the empty bottles. This is particularly creative pricing, but customers recognize the value and are willing to pay for it.

3. *Employ behavioral pricing.* A company has behavioral pricing opportunities when it wants to discourage its customers from acting in a certain way. This includes charging people a premium for custom services.

A health insurer found that one of its clients, a particularly large group of doctors, wanted to discuss invoice questions only on Fridays. The health insurer could do this only by dedicating a special "Friday team" at extra cost; it was able to charge the doctors' group for this custom service.

Airlines also use this type of pricing when people book tickets by phone rather than on the Internet. Every company I have worked with has similar types of opportunities.

4. *Employ market-based pricing.* With certain products or services, it is possible to charge one price in one geographic market and another price in a different one. Pricing becomes very complicated, as there are multiple price points for the same service. In these cases, companies are not always charging what the market will bear. They can increase prices just to match those of the competition.

There is no reason to confine the creativity released by breaking down barriers simply to reducing expenses. You would think that it would be particularly difficult for a utility to find new opportunities for revenue. Utilities are regulated and are prevented from raising prices to their customers in anything but a formal way, and they do just one thing: deliver something basic, such as water, electricity, or gas.

The employees of one utility company didn't feel those constraints. In their state, the utility was forced to replace customer meters every 20 years, whether they were faulty or not. But that restriction did not apply to utility companies in other states. By selling used meters to other utilities, rather than throwing them away, the company raised more than $250,000 in extra revenue a year—which it then passed back to its customers in terms of reduced prices.

Every company has huge opportunities to increase revenues. You often find that employees are more willing to come forward with expense-reduction ideas when a project focuses on both revenues and expenses. So, paradoxically, adding revenues to the equation means increased opportunity for reducing expenses.

Principle 10. The change process must not disrupt normal business.
This principle is a commitment I make to the companies I work with—
and a commitment they must make to themselves. If you are going
through a process of change, there is a time commitment to the process
itself, but you have to figure out ways to find this time while continuing
with business as usual.

Managers will have to delegate more, unnecessary activities may
be cut, and yes, some people will have to put in some extra work for
the one hundred days it takes to do a project. But it is critical that you
commit to this principle because most businesses don't have the luxury
of just shutting down for a period of time while a change process takes
place.

Companies keep this promise to themselves because they realize they
have to keep moving. I take pains to help companies make sure they can
meet their operational goals during the change process, as you will discover in chapter 11. At the beginning of a change project, the CEO typically states that while the project is running, despite how important it is,
everyone has to make sure that budgets for the next quarter and the length
of the project in particular get met.

In my experience, delegation to a trusted Number 2 is certainly possible for the short time it takes to do a project, but it is clearly not sustainable. On a number of occasions, I have seen a strange phenomenon—a
department actually improves when the manager is temporarily engaged
in breaking barriers. This happens when strong Number 2s step up to
show what they can do when given the chance. The improvement is not
sustainable, as the strong Number 2 cannot maintain the increased workload, but companies welcome it when it happens.

Principle 11. Implementation must be nothing less than 100 percent.
It sounds extreme to say that you should not accept anything less than
100 percent implementation, but that should be the expectation. And it
sounds unbelievable that following these principles often brings about
greater-than-expected results. But this is normally the case.

There are six reasons why expectations about the results should be so high.

1. The ideas have been decided using fact-based analysis, so the costs and implications of any decision are already known before an idea is implemented.
2. The ideas are owned by the managers of the departments who are affected by them, so there is not only buy-in but also championing of the ideas.
3. The ideas have been publicly committed to.
4. The ideas are tracked by a system that not only keeps managers honest and focused but also provides an early warning if an idea starts to go off track.
5. The impact of the ideas has been conservatively estimated so that many of the ideas actually produce more impact than was planned. It is for this very reason that a typical project I work on produces 102 percent of the planned impact.
6. If a particular idea goes off track, a manager is expected to replace the value of the idea. Managers commit to the impact of an idea, even if that idea is derailed through no fault of their own. They have ways to do this readily at hand, either by capturing more impact than planned from other ideas or by implementing extra ideas on which consensus had not been built or that were previously considered too risky. Managers have an idea bank to dig into if the value of their ideas falls short of expectations.

Project participants cannot say with absolute certainty, "Oh, three years from now, these 200 ideas will be implemented," because sometimes specific ideas may become hard to execute. Perhaps a regulation changes or some unforeseen circumstance occurs. But the participants can commit to the impact that is to be achieved, even if they have to find another way to reach the goal.

In the projects I have run, ideas do not get abandoned very often; I can still remember the five ideas (out of 700) that did not work at a company I worked with more than ten years ago. I know exactly why they didn't work, and I know the ideas that replaced them. But when an idea doesn't work, you must still expect 100 percent implementation in terms of financial impact.

Once people commit to ideas, they are not allowed to change their minds. And a manager who replaces one who committed to ideas cannot renege on his or her predecessor's commitments. The new manager is expected to commit to and deliver the same impact as his or her predecessor.

12. The change process must be about culture change, not just a completed project.

This is perhaps the most difficult principle to execute against because it is about changing the way people do things not just during the course of the project but also once it is completed. If culture change does not happen, the behavioral changes that occurred during the project are not sustainable. A number of things help to drive culture change within an organization. Some occur naturally with a focused project; others have to be driven into the organization. Here are the things a senior management team needs to do to drive culture change in an organization:

1. *Stress the importance of the project to the organization.* The focus and intensity of a project will lead employees to believe that it is important to the organization. If the goal of a highly visible project is to take complexity out of the organization, the workforce will naturally come to believe that simplicity is a focus for the organization. Striving for less complexity gains a foothold as part of the corporate culture.

2. *Emphasize the logic behind the change in culture.* Again using complexity as an example, employees will need to understand why it is

important to be less complex and why change must happen now. Sometimes a "burning bridge" makes the logic self-evident; in other cases, it will need to be explained. In both cases, employees need to understand why there is a sudden drive toward reduced complexity.

3. *Communicate your expectations continuously and frequently.* The more your colleagues hear from you about your expectations, the more they begin to believe in those expectations. Saying that we want to be "simpler" actually works—provided it is said over and over again. Tie every message to your colleagues back to the statement of simplicity.

4. *Lead by example.* Publicly demonstrating your passion for less complexity and how you yourself have taken steps to remove it will influence your colleagues.

5. *Expose good and bad examples—examples of both simplicity and complexity—in the organization.* Publicly praise and give accolades to those employees who have simplified the way they work. Highlighting egregious areas of complexity and asking (after several attempts to change behavior), "Why do we still do this?" also help to drive home culture change.

6. *Introduce new organizational language that describes the new culture.* One project I worked on was called "Innovate." People quickly started asking whether a process or a department had been "Innovated" yet.

7. *Change compensation systems.* Think of ways of rewarding the results of new behavior, either through regular compensation and bonus systems or with ad hoc programs. Rewards are a fast way to change a culture. Among your direct reports, it might be something as simple as a $500 reward for each idea that is implemented to simplify the organization. Whether you pay out one reward or fifty, you have people's attention. They quickly learn what behavior is important to you and the organization.

As the change in culture begins to kick in, you will begin to see small signs of behavioral change. Perhaps a manager will question why there are so many people at a particular meeting, why they are traveling to it, or why the meeting is even taking place. Perhaps another manager will question the length or frequency of a particular report—or whether it is even needed.

Much to my chagrin, I also see this culture change having an impact on the change process. Over the years, most elements of the process have been tried and tested. But as their newfound passion for efficiency takes hold, it is not unusual for my former clients to begin to question if I can make the change process itself simpler or more efficient!

CHAPTER 10

IT'S ALL ABOUT PSYCHOLOGY

OUR PROJECT AT A HUGE AND SUCCESSFUL GLOBAL company was led on a day-to-day basis by a veteran who had been with the company for more than 20 years. He knew where a lot of the ideas were buried within the organization, and he was beginning to get very excited because for the first time in his tenure, the company was actually doing something to address all the issues the company had. "The real difference, George, is that this process doesn't tell you what to do or how to do it," I said to him one day. "It doesn't tell you why or when or even that you should make specific changes. What it does do very well is that it creates the environment for change. I like to tell my clients that it is 75 percent about psychology."

"You're wrong, Neil," he said. "It is 90 percent about psychology." And he was absolutely right.

You might think that the most difficult part of a change process is getting enough good ideas out on the table, but in fact that turns out to be the easiest part. Although it is a surprise to most people, there are literally thousands of ideas (big and small) in every company. Once you ask for them, they come. It is like opening the floodgates. Earlier we asked you to think about your own company. How long did it take *you* to come up with ten ideas for improvement in your company? My guess is that it was a pretty easy exercise.

The real challenge is a completely different one. Companies are made up of human beings—people just like you and me. They are given specific roles and responsibilities. But they also bring with them many different personalities. Some are collaborative and others confrontational, some are risk takers and some are risk averse; there are innovators and implementers, doers and thinkers, those who are creative and those who are practical.

Companies benefit hugely from this diversity, as weaknesses in some employees are made up for by the strengths of others. What a good change process is really about is getting all of these different types of people to share the same focus for long enough to "play the game." A chief executive officer once asked me, "Do you think talking to people about 'playing the game' gives them the wrong idea? I don't want them to think that we're not looking for real buy-in from them." I explained to him that I use that phrase to remind people that the process is about *participation*. They cannot be spectators to this change process.

Managing people is a difficult task. As every leader knows, it is about keeping them motivated, and you cannot do that simply by instructing your team and micromanaging. People have to be able to make their own decisions in their own way and in their own time. They are hired to do just that. But the dilemma is that those decisions need to be consistent with the goals the company is trying to achieve.

"Playing the game" in the context of change means the following:

- Everyone must be included in the process; no part of a company can be allowed not to play.
- Managers can't delegate the process because it is not a high enough priority for them.
- Managers can't ignore the process, thinking or hoping it doesn't really apply to them.
- Managers can't pretend to play while actually working against the process.
- Good ideas can't be hidden.
- Good ideas can't be undervalued.

The twelve principles presented in chapter 9 provide the rules of the game, and the process itself provides the framework. But the real challenge of a good change process is managing behavior. A good process seeks to identify early any of the errant behaviors just described, because each has the potential to undermine it. And then the change process seeks to correct the behavior. The process works gently at first, but if the behavior continues to exist, the process makes the transgressors highly visible.

Why would managers behave in a way that undermines a process that is embraced by the rest of the company and sponsored by the CEO? Surely, this seems almost certainly a career-limiting move. In my experience, I have seen a number of reasons.

Managers may believe that their own strategic priorities (often linked to generating revenues for the company) are more important than a change process. For example, in an investment bank, business leaders actually may need to be on the trading floor every day when the markets are open, generating revenue and protecting assets. They can't miss that obligation just to participate in a change project. Managers in a bank's risk area may feel that regulatory scrutiny makes the task they do so important that they couldn't possibly spend time thinking about a change process. Every company has its own critical lifeblood functions and those who run them may feel they take priority over a change process.

Other managers may feel that they have amassed enough "capital" within the company not to play. It is not their game; someone else thought it up, and they are personally too important to be included or to give the process the time it needs. Typically, these managers have successfully excluded themselves from other corporate-wide initiatives in the past. Such managers might also claim, "There is no opportunity in my area. We are already as efficient as we can be."

TWENTY REASONS FOR KILLING GOOD IDEAS

1. Our company is well run; there are no opportunities.
2. We're inefficient, but my department is not the problem.
3. The issue is support functions and allocations, not my costs.

4. Our problem is revenues, not how we do things.

5. We have tried that before.

6. We are already doing that.

7. My boss / the CEO / legal will never agree to that.

8. That won't save money or increase revenues.

9. That would cost too much to implement.

10. No one in the industry is doing that.

11. We will lose customers if we do that.

12. Anything that takes time away from serving my customers will hurt us.

13. But we are unique.

14. No one really understands what we do.

15. I don't have time to think about that.

16. We don't have the right technology to do that.

17. I can't risk my job raising that.

18. I can only impact my own department.

19. I don't have the right people to do that.

20. Now is not a good time for us to make changes.

Managers might also want to avoid playing for another reason—because ideas are sometimes very difficult to do and, without a process, there is no pressure to resolve them. David, a Catalyst Team Member (CTM) at a recent client and one of the full-time employees dedicated to a project, described an experience that illustrates this point very well. David was charged with working with the global client's finance area—an area that he knew nothing about. The finance department already had outsourced many of its simple tasks to the company's Philippines-based operations, where labor was cheaper. Harry, the leader of the finance area, said to David, "I could send them a lot more, but the extra work would be much more complicated to do, and I'm reluctant to send it over there." David arranged a call between Rajan, the head of the Philippine operations, and Harry.

Harry explained that he had not moved the tasks because he would have to directly manage the employees to ensure their work was done correctly. "But why would you have to do that?" Rajan asked. "We operate many functions for different areas of the company and they all are managed locally. No one else in the company manages their Philippine employees; it is just far easier for us to do so."

About 27 minutes into the 30-minute call, David realized it wasn't going anywhere. "You both have good points, but let me get this right," he said. "You are going to tell Bob, the CEO, that our company could save $3 million a year on this idea, but he can't do it because you can't decide who manages these employees?" The issue was resolved in the next three minutes. It is not important which way management went; the point is that the managers were having difficulty resolving a tough issue that absent the process would have remained unresolved. But because of the process, they "played the game" and reached a decision with which they were both comfortable.

Each time I have carried out the PGI Promise® process, at least one senior manager has resisted it. And it is perfectly understandable that people are skeptical of anything new or different. (See the box on pages 160–161 that lists 20 common "reasons" managers give for not wanting to pursue a project.) But I always ask managers to keep an open mind and at least give the process a fair shot. What is there to lose? If I am proven right, enormous rewards may be gained.

I also encourage managers to embrace the change project in another way. It is very rare to have the entire organization focused in the same manner on the same thing at the same time. This is the chance for good managers to make things they want to happen actually happen. I suggest managers use the process to shape their department as they want it to be shaped. As one of my colleagues likes to say, because of our change process, the organization is "unfrozen" for a short space of time. This window provides a real opportunity to cut through the normal red tape to get things done. Smart managers figure out how to use the process to their advantage.

Influential managers in companies that undertake a change process also have another challenge. It is important that they "play the game," but this alone is not sufficient. They need to *embrace* the project outwardly and visibly. As soon as a change process starts, the direct reports of an influential manager immediately try to determine if he or she really supports it. And it is not what managers say publicly that counts. What counts is their body language and what they do or don't do.

The direct reports of an influential manager typically are ferociously supportive and loyal. The manager is their protector and sometimes their mentor; typically they follow the manager's views and take their cues from him or her. When a new project is sprung on them, they watch their manager's behavior to figure out how they should respond to the project and how high it should be on their priority list. If it is right for the manager, it will be right for the direct reports.

Sometimes senior managers progress through three stages of denial before they can entirely endorse the process:

> Stage 1. "We are very strong [in many cases, the company is an industry leader]. We don't have any opportunity."
>
> Stage 2. "I can certainly now see that there is opportunity, but it's not in my area. It's in everybody else's area, particularly in the support or overhead units."
>
> Stage 3. "Sure, there is some opportunity in my area, but it's mostly on the revenue side. That's what we should be focusing on, not cutting costs."

During a change process, leaders also have to be on their guard in a completely different way. There can be no inquests around previous inactions. The CEO of a food manufacturer was sitting through a review, listening to his team present ideas for change. The company used the FIFO (first in, first out) method for controlling inventory. Inventory that was produced first would be used first, so the company would not be left with inventory that went past its expiration date.

The same process was also used for frozen foods, but it was very difficult to implement there. There was limited space in the cold store to move the pallets of food around, but under the FIFO system, the new ones had to be put at the back and the old ones had to be put at the front. More important, a quick analysis showed that the FIFO method wasn't necessary here. The shelf life of frozen food is a lot longer than the shelf life of other foods; there was virtually no danger that the frozen food would be kept in-house past its sell-by date. The cold store employees generated a very good idea to stop the FIFO system in their area, which would mean they could then reduce staff in their area because inventory would not be moved around as frequently.

When this idea was presented, Ron, the CEO, immediately left the room. I went chasing after him to find out what was wrong. This was a great idea; why did he have such a bad reaction to it? "We supposedly stopped using FIFO in the cold store five years ago," he said. "I am furious!" He probably had a right to be furious, but he couldn't let his emotions show. "Ron, there can be no inquests in this process," I reminded him. "If you don't have an amnesty, people will be afraid to raise good ideas for fear of what your reaction might be." To his credit, Ron immediately returned to the room and praised his managers for their excellent "new" idea. I think this incident clearly demonstrates why one of the rules of a good change process is that there can be no inquests. Managers, including the CEO, cannot reprimand people for not taking actions earlier.

The test of a good change process is whether it manages the people in the organization, including its leaders. The process will feel very uncomfortable for many in the organization. They will not be used to going through something like this on a day-to-day basis. Ideas will be released in droves, and the process will run like clockwork; the unknown—the part of the process that requires the greatest management—is the behavior of the participants and their reactions to the process. George was absolutely right when he said an excellent process is 90 percent about psychology. My mantra to participants is, "Trust the process."

CHAPTER 11

A 100-DAY PROCESS FOR BREAKING BARRIERS

BEFORE I BEGIN DESCRIBING THE THREE-STEP PROCESS that has developed from my work over the last 20 years, let me say that I don't believe it is the only one that will break down barriers. But it is one that I know works because of the success that companies have had using no less than 5 different versions of it, each with minor variations, over the years. I make my clients A Promise (the acronym for the barriers): if our process doesn't help the company save money, increase profits, and reduce complexity, we work for free. I am glad to say it is a promise that I have never had to make good on.

We have already looked at the eight barriers to change and the twelve principles that must govern an effective change process. And we have discovered that psychology is the key to making the process work. Remember, the overarching belief is that within any company, even the most highly successful, the opportunity exists to dramatically improve performance *using internal resources*. Those internal resources are the employees and their ideas for reducing complexity, improving profitability, and growing revenue. Throughout this process, their ideas will be surfaced, valued, risk rated, and debated, so that people who commit to them can do so with conviction and confidence.

We set a one-hundred-working-day timeline for this three-step project. At the end of those one hundred days, there is a commitment by managers company-wide to the changes they will make and what the financial impact will be. Most changes will not be implemented or even begun by that time, but an implementation plan and a tracking system will be in place. All ideas must be implemented within 36 months; 60 to 70 percent will be implemented within the first year.

A successful change process has been used in companies that have tens of thousands of employees and many divisions, as well as in smaller, less complex organizations with fewer than 3,000 employees. One of the reasons I believe it has been successful in organizations of all sizes and types is that the principles are universally applicable and usually strictly followed. They are all important, but one of the key principles of the PGI Promise® is: "The entire organization must be involved." No division is singled out or favored, and just as important, no division is left out or overlooked. Meaningful change cannot be achieved unless the process is fair and inclusive.

The process works best when it is applied to an entire company and its multiple divisions that interact with each other, but it can also work with a single department. In that case, ideas that cut across departments cannot be considered so the impact will be less. However, the process can still be done. We discuss results of a good change process in detail in chapter 12, but it guarantees to rid the company of its barriers. And it changes the company's culture. Sustainability only comes about, however, if the culture change is reinforced and supported. Companies have to take additional measures to make culture change stick and to prevent barriers from creeping back.

OVERVIEW OF OUR PROCESS

The process that I use to break barriers is called the PGI Promise®. It builds directly from the twelve principles and is designed to create the environment that is necessary for change.

The process has three major steps, and each one culminates in a review meeting before senior management. Step 1 (leading up to the first review) is all about surfacing ideas and putting together a comprehensive portfolio of ideas, organized into themes. Step 2 (and moving into the second review) is about valuing, risk rating, and debating those ideas. Step 3 is about building consensus around the ideas that the company wants to move forward with, which leads into the third and final review at which decisions are made. At the end of Step 3, a two-week implementation planning period transitions into the implementation phase.

Baseline	How much money the Group spends today.
Cross-Group Topic	A large idea that goes across Groups.
CTL	Catalyst Team Leader—liaison between SCMs and CTMs.
CTM	Catalyst Team Member—full-time on project working with Groups they are not from.
GL	Group Leader—natural leader of a business or an area that becomes a project Group.
Group	A natural area of the business which becomes the everyday unit in the project. Collectively all Groups add up to the entire company.
ICs	Implementation Coordinators—small team of CTMs who stay after the project's 100 days to track implementation.
Idea	An action under control of the GL that reduces costs or increases revenues and can be implemented in a defined time (usually 36 months).
Ideas	Specific actions that will be valued and rated.
Risk Rating	Level of risk of an idea—either Low, Medium, or High.
SCM	Steering Committee Member.
SCR	Steering Committee Review; Group Leaders present to the Steering Committee at 3 reviews.
Topics	Categories into which ideas are organized.
Valuation	Economic value of an idea.

EXHIBIT 11.1   Terminology

Before describing each of the steps in more detail, it is helpful to explain the three types of participants who will be instrumental in making the process work; some of the key concepts of our process, such as the timeline and baselines; and some terminology. Along the way, you will see the principles coming into play. Also, bear in mind that although I am describing the process here as it applies to an entire organization, the same structure and concepts apply equally to a department or division.

This description of the process is organized in the following way:

A. Participants

B. Timeline

C. Groups and baselines

D. Other key concepts

E. Preplanning (Step 0)

F. Surfacing ideas (Step 1)

G. Valuing, risk rating, and debating (Step 2)

H. Building consensus (Step 3)

I. Implementation planning

J. Ensuring 100 percent implementation

K. The role of the project partners

A. PARTICIPANTS

While the entire organization will be involved in the process, three main types of participants drive the process. They are the Catalyst Team Members (CTMs), the Steering Committee Members (SCMs), and the Group Leaders (GLs). There is also a Catalyst Team Leader and a small Support group. The participants shown in Exhibit 11.2.

Catalyst Team Members

Your process should begin by taking the organization and dividing it up into "Groups"—the units around which the process will be organized. The Groups will likely follow the normal everyday structure of the organization—sales, marketing, manufacturing, servicing, finance, and human resources (HR) may be some of the areas that are designated as Groups. Depending on the size of the company, there may be 25 to 50

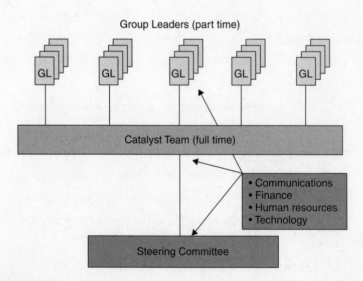

EXHIBIT 11.2 Participants

such Groups. During the process, each Group will look at one area of the company; there is no overlap. Together, the Groups constitute the entire company.

CTMs are high-level people drawn from across the organization who are assigned full time to the project for its entire one hundred days. They are often thought of as superstars; they are people who typically cannot be spared. Their selection in itself sends a message from senior management to the organization: "We are serious about this project. Look who we have freed up to do it."

I worked with one bank where all of the senior executives were sacrificing some of their strongest performers to be CTMS, with one exception. One key executive clearly wasn't buying into the process, and he designated less-than-stellar people for CTMs. Once his peers saw this, their original choices for CTMs suddenly had other more important work to do, and the selections became increasingly diluted in terms of skill. The chief financial officer of the company saw what was going on and went to the CEO. "We have one chance to do this right," he said. "We need to free up the key people." The CEO was wise and figured out how to make it work. "I can see that," he said. "But I'll make you a deal. I will get the right resources on the project if you lead it on a day-to-day basis." The CFO could see the value to the company and readily agreed to lead the project. To this day, he is happy that he did. When the huge results of the project became clear, he was delighted to be known as the senior executive who sponsored it.

The CTMs work in pairs and are intentionally assigned to areas they are not from and know nothing about. Their stature and reputation in the organization gives them credibility; their lack of expertise in the areas they are assigned to work in gives them freedom to question everything. They can ask "dumb" questions and get away with it. In this way, creative thinking is introduced into the project organization at the highest level.

The CTMs collectively represent all major areas and all major geographies of the company. They relocate to a "war room" environment without the trappings of their normal roles. Cubicles are substituted for offices; there is no space for their assistants. Each pair of CTMs manages three to four Groups, so there are typically about 20 CTMs on a project. Of course this is a range, depending on the size of the company and the number of Groups; one small project using an early version of the process had just 8 CTMs while one large global project had 55 CTMs spread over 4 locations.

The CTMs work with the Groups to guide them on the process but, more important, to challenge their thinking about the way things are done today within the Group. CTMs also fulfill one other very important function. They coordinate the "Cross-Group Topics" that cut across organizational lines. Such opportunities can account for more than 60 percent of the impact in any project.

The selection of CTMs is an important task for any senior management team and involves a series of meetings. You cannot pull out *all* of the superstars—the organization still has to function for the one hundred days that the CTMs devote to the process. You can include a limited number of more junior CTMs who are rising within the organization and who would benefit from the exposure a project gives.

As we discussed in chapter 9, usually in a good change process it is reasonably straightforward to select two-thirds of the team, but for the remaining third, tough choices about priorities have to be made. You will recall that sometimes a strange phenomenon occurs: the area where the CTM is from actually produces better results when the person is removed. In these cases, lower-level managers are proving how well they can do in the boss's absence; usually, however, the improvement is not sustainable because people cannot manage the increased workload indefinitely. In chapter 9, we described the four major qualities that each CTM must display:

1. Intelligence
2. The ability to be a team player
3. A passion for change
4. The ability to get things done

The process has a number of side benefits for the senior executives who select the CTMs. They get to see how their next management generation—the CTMs—can perform in unfamiliar settings where they have no experience. They can also see how well succession plans are working by focusing on the people who will fill in for the CTMs for one hundred days. Managers who were strong in their normal role can be surprisingly weak CTMs. And CTMs who were put on the team as a test can excel. Being a member of the Catalyst Team can make careers. As I mentioned, at least three former CTMs involved in change processes have gone on to be CEOs in their own right.

Steering Committee Members

The CEO and the most senior management of the organization form the Steering Committee (SC). Together they set the tone for the project and act as its champions. Although the project is very visible within the organization, it will take a minimal amount of their time. Most of that time will be spent in Steering Committee Reviews (SCRs)—the three review sessions at which the Groups present, in turn, their ideas to the SCMs.

If 50 Groups are presenting their portfolios of ideas for change, each SCR can take up to three days. While this amount of time may seem daunting, almost every SCM I have worked with has found these meetings compelling. With the complexity and speed involved in running a company in today's environment, it is very difficult for any manager to have a complete grasp of what is going on throughout the organization. The reviews provide a unique opportunity for the management team to learn exactly how the company works and how each part of it comes together, as well as to listen to thousands of ideas for improvement.

One CEO of an insurance company I worked with had seen the data that showed people who voluntarily left the company tended to do so early in the new year. But he didn't know why.

When he sat through his first SCR, he quickly realized the reason for the annual January exodus. The company's policy regarding vacations and voluntary departures (which he had inherited when he took over) was very generous. Provided employees worked just one day of the new year, they would get paid for a full year of vacation days when they left the firm. Not surprisingly, no one left October through December, and there was a spike in resignations at the end of the first week in January. There was no way the CEO could have known the details of the leaving policy—it was too much detail too low in the organization.

While SCMs have genuine input and influence and a fairly firm say over ideas that are going to be implemented, much of their contribution to the project is in showing support for the change process.

Group Leaders and Associate Group Leaders

Each Group is led by a "Group Leader" (GL) who is more than likely the head of that business unit. GLs are accountable for their own business area in the process. Associate Group Leaders (AGLs) are selected by the GLs from among the ranks of the Group to help them.

The GL role is not full time on a project; GLs are expected to maintain their current responsibilities throughout the one hundred days of the project. In addition to their normal work, they are responsible for the results of the project in their area. They will present their ideas for change three times at each of the SCRs. Before the end of the project, GLs need to generate or solicit ideas for change in their area, determine the impact of those changes, figure out which changes they want to do, and advocate for them.

Sometimes the changes will require fact gathering or analysis before they can be considered. And they may affect other people. The GL's job is also to get input from others. After the project has finished, GLs are responsible for implementing the ideas that they have advocated, which everyone else has agreed to, and which management has approved.

The GL role can be a tough one. The project work is clearly important to the company; it will bring results in terms of reduced complexity, a changed culture, and a huge financial impact. But it can put a strain on the GLs who, unless they manage the role well, will have extra work to do. The GLs are helped by the fact that the change project is short—it lasts only one hundred days. And there are two other things that GLs can do to help manage the extra workload:

1. A good manager needs to delegate activities—GLs must delegate to the AGLs within the project and to their direct reports for their regular activities.
2. GLs need to temporarily rearrange their own priorities by reducing or delaying some of the tasks they are currently undertaking. After all, not many tasks have a higher priority than dramatically improving the company's profits.

Although participation is a challenge, in all the years I have been doing these process I have seldom found a GL who was not up to the task.

Catalyst Team Leader

One of the SCMs plays the role of Catalyst Team Leader (CTL), a liaison between the Catalyst Team and the Steering Committee. Typically, this is not a full-time role, but it can be one. Although the project is really driven by the CEO and the senior management team, the CTL acts as a project sponsor. The CTL is the person who resolves issues on a day-to-day basis and keeps the project on track. He or she is the go-to person for any issues or questions related to the project and is responsible for making sure it runs smoothly. As the project sponsor, the CTL can contribute ideas, although his or her ideas have no more weight than anyone else's. And the CTL is not involved in implementation; once the project is over, the CTL will go back to his or her previous job.

Support Teams

A small number of teams across the organization support the efforts of the Steering Committee, the Catalyst Team, and the Group Leaders. Finance plays a role in setting up the project by developing baselines, leading any rebudgeting that needs to be done after the project is complete, and tracking the results. Communications helps to develop a rationale for the project and helps prepare the messages for the project kickoff, both internally and externally. During the project, the communications team keeps the employees up to speed with progress. At the end, it drafts internal and external communications announcing the results.

A small technology team also has a role in the project. A number of the ideas for change will involve a technology component. It is the task of this tech team to figure out the investment cost of the technology resources needed to implement such ideas. And finally, the HR team typically becomes involved at the back end of a project to create a forward-looking personnel plan.

B. TIMELINE

Over the years, I have tried to make the change process in the projects I have led as short and efficient as possible while still maintaining its integrity. When I first started doing this work in the early 1990s, a project contained five reviews and lasted nine months. I began to realize this was too long when a senior executive joined a client just after the project started— and left before it finished. You just cannot keep organizational attention on anything for that long a period—no matter how important it is. So now the process takes just one hundred days.

Before the one-hundred-day project can begin, there is a six- to eight-week period of low-key preplanning to organize for it. I sometimes call this Step 0. The project starts the day the CTMs come on board full time and finishes the day they leave.

The project is broken into three steps. Step 1, the idea-surfacing phase, lasts just four weeks. Steps 2 and 3, in which the ideas are valued, risk rated, and debated, and in which consensus is built around any controversial ideas, are the core of the project, lasting ten weeks combined. Before the CTMs leave the project, there are two weeks of implementation planning. Although these steps are described as linear, they are not really so. Surfacing ideas can take place any time during the project, although the majority of it happens in Step 1. And if an idea is easy to value, there is no reason to wait until Step 2 to do so. (These steps are shown in Exhibit 11.3.)

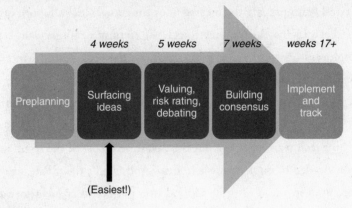

EXHIBIT 11.3 Timeline

C. GROUPS AND BASELINES

As we have seen, the organizational units of the project are called Groups and a Group Leader heads each. There are two basic types of Groups—those that focus on ideas to reduce costs and those that focus on ideas to increase revenues. We keep these Groups separate because we have found it is too great a temptation to focus just on revenues. Growing a company (generating more revenues) is always more exciting than shrinking it (reducing the costs), so we want to make sure that reducing costs gets the attention it deserves. We do this by having dedicated Groups that look only at costs.

Keeping GLs focused (and making sure there is no duplication of effort) is critical in a process that is so short. Another method used to keep GLs focused mandates that GLs can spend time saving money only in their own area. Does this mean that a GL cannot come up with ideas for change in other areas? Of course not. Those ideas are welcome, and the process needs them.

But using the principle that it is easy to get an idea into the process but hard to remove it, ideas are tramsferred to their relevant Groups, which is where they will be evaluated and where the financial impact will be counted. In this way, GLs focus on saving money in their own areas, not in other people's areas. GLs get credit only for those savings suggested in their own area—or received from others about their area.

Each Group has a "baseline," which is a way of measuring where the Group is today. For cost Groups, the baseline is how much money the Group spends today. For revenue Groups, it is how much revenue the Group generates today. The baseline is helpful in a number of ways:

- *The baseline prevents duplication.* It prevents more than one person working on the same savings. The baseline defines the "sandbox" in which the GL can play. The GL is responsible for generating ideas that affect only his or her baseline.
- *The baseline can help to focus the GL's efforts.* The baseline gives an idea of how money is currently being spent within the Group. If the Group is spending a lot of money on travel, for example, the GL knows that he or she can save money by looking for travel-related ideas.
- *The baseline helps to provide a measure of how well a Group is doing in a project.* By measuring the amount of revenue generated or the amount of cost saved as a percentage of a Group's baseline, the Group's relative performance can be measured by the SCMs. Is this a 5 percent Group or a 15 percent Group?
- *The baseline can also help the GL to value ideas.* How much can be saved by taking a certain action?

What if an idea saves money in more than one Group's baseline? In these cases, each Group can consider the idea. In finalizing the baselines, there is another rule that project participants really like. They are responsible only for generating ideas for change across the costs they control (so-called direct costs). In this process, they are not responsible for any allocations—costs that are passed to them by another department. Those costs go to the originating Group to make savings against.

The baseline contains not just the dollars that the organization spends but also the positions in the organization. Each position and each person is assigned to one Group—and only one Group. The challenge for the GL is also to come up with ideas to see if people's time can be saved or put to better use.

D. OTHER KEY CONCEPTS

Ideas

In this book, we talk continually about "ideas," but what *is* an idea? Early on in our process, we tend to hear not ideas but statements and descriptions of problems. For example: "We can't provide the customer service we want to on Fridays because the volume of calls increases on that day." Somewhere in this statement there probably is an idea to make an improvement, but it is well hidden. The idea might be, "Staff up on Fridays to meet peak customer service demand and staff down at slow times."

Another early suggestion might be, "Fire Joe because he is useless at his job." In our process, this does not count as an idea—you cannot have ideas that are focused on individuals, regardless of how accurate they are.

Yet another common early idea is to transfer the cost of doing something to someone else. But if the transfer does not involve any savings to the company (rather than the Group), it is not an idea in our process. Cost cannot just be passed to someone else.

As the term is used in our process, an "idea" has four key characteristics:

1. It describes an action, not a problem.
2. The action can be taken by the GL (and is not in someone else's control).
3. The action either saves at least some costs or increases at least some revenues in the GL's Group (and not elsewhere).
4. The idea can be completely implemented in a defined period (usually 36 months).

> Rather surprisingly, most ideas do not involve changes in technology. Fewer than 10 percent of approved ideas have a technology-related implementation cost.

With these rules in place, it is easy to determine what is an idea and what is not an idea.

Valuing

Every idea will have a value—that is, the costs it saves or the revenues it generates, stated on an annual basis. The process has certain rules so that all ideas are valued in the same way and so that ideas have a short "payback"; that is, the costs to implement them are quickly recovered. The GL calculates the value because he or she is the one who will be expected to capture that value when the idea is implemented.

Risk Rating

Every idea that comes into the system will be risk rated by the relevant GL, the CTM, and anyone else the idea affects. GLs cannot prevent an idea from being considered, but they can say how risky the ideas might be. Risk can be measured on a number of dimensions: the risk of losing customers, the risk of implementation, and legal risk are just three types. Risk raters have three choices: Low, Medium, and High. The goal of the process is to build consensus around an idea by reducing the risk associated with it.

Steering Committee Reviews

Every Group goes before the SCMs three times, once at the end of each step, to present their ideas. Each SCR happens over the course of two to three days, so each Group generally has only 20 to 30 minutes to present its ideas. In the first review, the SC should not only get a good sense of each Group's portfolio of ideas but also test each GL's commitment to the process. This is not the time for debate. The SCMs will ask questions, but the goal is to keep the review moving quickly.

At the second review, the SCMs will discuss the big and controversial ideas presented by the GLs. The third review is for decision making. By that time ideas will have been discussed multiple times, consensus will have been built, and the GLs and SCMs will know what they want to approve—and what they want to turn down.

E. PREPLANNING (STEP 0)

I am serious when I say the whole organization has to be engaged in the project because the entire company is going to be looked at, and a lot of behind-the-scenes preparation work is involved in making that possible.

One of the first steps in preplanning is to develop a communications plan to explain to the organization what is about to happen and to enlist everyone's help. The first thing to develop, if it does not naturally exist, is a rationale for doing the project. This happens during the preplanning phase, and the first draft is created by the communications team for discussion with the SCMs. Employees will want to know why this project is important to the company and why it is important *now*. The best rationale is crafted in such a way that a barrier-breaking project is seen as the next logical step for the company to take. It should fit right in with the company's strategy. Explaining this logic should not be difficult—it should be the next logical step.

During the preplanning phase, the SCMs also design the Groups and select the CTMs and the GLs. They select the CTMs over a number of weeks, by creating a pool and then narrowing it down. Each SCM is expected to contribute strong players to the pool, although, of course, not all of them will be selected. This task is about balancing the need for a small number of strong CTMs to assign to a project with the need to leave strong people to run the business as usual. The GLs are usually preselected automatically by virtue of their role in the organization—they are the natural heads of the Groups.

During this phase, the small finance team establishes the initial baselines for each GL. The GLs will have the chance to question the baselines later, but the initial round of forming the Groups' baselines takes place during the preplanning stage. The HR team also assigns organizational positions to each of the Groups.

F. SURFACING IDEAS (STEP 1)

In the first part of the process, much of the activity is around collecting, organizing, and sifting and sorting ideas. The goal is a clean portfolio of ideas that covers all costs or revenues of the Group.

Surfacing ideas is (perhaps surprisingly) the easiest part of the change process, and in some ways it is the most exciting. Once effective communications about the project have been launched, people are enthusiastic and eager to get involved. They recognize that this is their chance to be heard and to make a difference. (This is especially true for people lower down in the organization who generally lack influence or a conduit to management.)

You will quickly find that there is no shortage of ideas in your organization. You will probably be surprised by how many good ideas there are, how many are duplicated, and how many have surfaced before. In fact, you are likely to find that more than 75 percent of the ideas have been proposed before in one form or another. The huge number of ideas is in part due to the new company-wide systems for collecting them but mostly due to the fact that many employees will view this as "their chance" to air their ideas and to say what they think.

Don't think that people are being lazy or truculent in bringing up ideas that have already been rejected. Shrewd GLs and other employees recognize this process as a second chance for ideas they genuinely believe in. Think of the process as "liberating" ideas that have been wrongly buried. At the very least, people can be assured that their ideas won't be eliminated because someone wants to Avoid Controversy, is Reluctant to Change, or is a Management Blocker.

The number of times you receive an idea is probably a pretty good indicator of a lingering problem that needs a resolution.

By SCR 1, which marks the end of the four weeks of Step 1, a GL's goal is to have developed a complete and comprehensive portfolio of ideas with the promise of strong financial savings and changing the way the Group is doing business. GLs and their teams will have done the following:

- Confirmed that their baseline is correct
- Generated hundreds if not thousands of ideas that affect their Group
- Removed duplicates and organized those ideas by topic

- Attached rough value and assigned an initial risk rating to each idea
- Figured out which key analyses they need to do

Rules and Methods for Surfacing Ideas

In order to promote creativity and to get every idea on the table, a number of rules govern idea generation.

1. All areas of an organization are encouraged to participate by surfacing and submitting ideas; no area is excluded, and no topic cannot be explored.
2. Any employee can submit ideas concerning any part of the organization.
3. An idea can be removed from the process only if it is not really an idea or if it is a duplicate. Each idea undergoes a rigorous CTM review before it is removed.
4. Every idea that is submitted will be considered, but it is not possible to tell employees what happened to their individual ideas.

GLs can encourage people to provide ideas in three major ways: solicitation, brainstorming, and problem solving. Each of these methods has its strengths, and each is especially useful in its own way.

Idea solicitation is about casting the widest possible net. There are no restrictions: this is simply asking anyone in the organization to come up with ideas for change and send them in to the CTMs through a number of channels—email, voicemail, filling in a form, sending in a letter. The ideas can be left openly or anonymously, and they can affect the employee's part of the organization or any other. This method gets the process started and generates organization-wide enthusiasm and activity. By volume, most ideas will come in during the solicitation process.

Occasionally, the solicitation process unearths a huge opportunity; in general, however, the sum of all these ideas is likely to account for only 20 percent of the financial impact. Nevertheless, asking for these ideas (and committing to consider them) is critical in terms of simplifying what the organization does and in terms of winning organizational support for change. Once the request is made, the ideas will flow in. One company I worked with found that ideas continued to pour in at a rate of 45 a day even *after* their project had finished.

Ideas that come through solicitation are assigned by the CTMs to the Group that would be impacted by the idea. At this stage, as long as a suggestion meets the criteria for an idea, it will be considered. While the complete database of ideas is available only to the project participants, companies can share some of the submitted ideas company-wide to create transparency and encourage more ideas.

Brainstorming is the best approach to get a Group to generate as many ideas as possible in one session. The target might be one hundred ideas in an hour. There is a focus, and the focus can be either broad ("Let's brainstorm about the way we sell to our customers") or deep ("Let's brainstorm about ways we can reduce our travel expenses"). But during a brainstorming session, there is no time to discuss or debate the ideas that come up; the goal is merely to record them and move forward. Flip charts are filled and scribes are busy in these sessions.

Everyone is encouraged to speak, present an idea, and move on. The most innovative ideas may come out of brainstorming. People are not taking the time to explain their ideas in detail, so there is opportunity for everyone to speak.

STEERING COMMITTEE MEMBER BRAINSTORMING

The entire organization will be asked to contribute ideas, including senior management. Not surprisingly, I have found that some of the most high-impact ideas come from senior management. This is just one of the reasons I find it valuable for SCMs to go through brainstorming sessions at the same time as they are being conducted throughout the rest of the organization. Not only do SCMs get to contribute ideas with the same "freedom" as the rest of the organization, but by participating in the process, they also get some insight into what is happening in Groups all across the company.

To the brainstorming session, each SCM should bring a dozen ideas for change that relate to his or her own area, as well as a dozen that are *outside* his or her own area. SCMs will be asked to share their ideas at the session in round-robin fashion. At this time, ideas can be clarified but should not be debated. However, they can be upgraded either to make them easier to implement or to increase their impact. The SC ideas are included in the process anonymously so that they are considered on their merits and not because they are SC ideas.

A good brainstorming session is like making popcorn. At first there is silence, then you hear a few kernels popping before there is the nonstop rat-a-tat of hot kernels exploding, and then things quiet down again. Once a brainstorming session really takes off, the ideas start flying fast and furious. People feed off of each other's enthusiasm and build on each other's ideas.

Problem solving is best suited for big, complex ideas and the more controversial ones, many of which are already well-known and may have been floated before. Sessions should be highly focused around very specific topics, and the participants should all be very knowledgeable about the issue, know why the complex idea has not been implemented, and have a strong, informed point of view. In short, they are the "experts" on this topic. Problem-solving sessions are designed to come up with solutions to big ideas that have not been implemented. Often the biggest project ideas are resolved in these sessions. The goal of these sessions is for focused debate around how an idea can be implemented.

GLs also can start the ideas flowing by looking at past ideas that were not implemented and by encouraging teams to rethink the way they currently do their jobs. Talking to senior managers and employees who have been with the organization for a long time will be especially useful in drawing out those ideas that have already been suggested and rejected. If possible, GLs should find out why the ideas were rejected, as this information will be useful in risk rating and building consensus.

When a Group starts working on surfacing ideas, it is helpful to have a small number of broad topics—say, ten—that cover all the Group's areas of costs (or revenue if it is a revenue-generating Group). Looking at the baseline will help GLs be sure that the topic list is comprehensive. Topics help in identifying areas where ideas are missing and in surfacing new ideas. Having broad topics is also essential in organizing ideas to facilitate discussion with the Steering Committee.

Some general themes to explore to help generate ideas (see Exhibit 11.4) include reducing the complexity and volume of the work, streamlining processes, moving work to more junior people, changing the structure of an organization, and de-layering management. There is a logic to the order of these themes. Early in our process, GLs are tempted to automate many manual processes, but automation should be one of the final steps. You do not want to automate an inefficient process—you want to make the process efficient before considering automation. Similarly, GLs find that they can save money by outsourcing a process rather than fixing it. But when the process is fixed, the economics change, and often outsourcing no longer makes sense. Automation and outsourcing should not be considered until all other themes have been pursued.

Groups that are focused on generating revenue work in parallel to the cost Groups and look at ways to raise revenues from existing products, services, and customers. As we saw in chapter 9, there are four broad areas

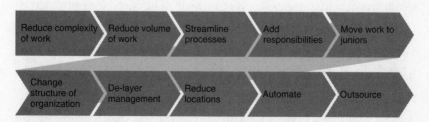

EXHIBIT 11.4   Themes to Explore When Generating Ideas

for increasing revenues: stopping leakage, behavioral pricing, pricing for value, and market-based pricing.

During Step 1, GLs are asked to concentrate specifically on their own Groups and not on coordinating ideas across Groups; Cross-Group activity will comprise much of the later stages of the process. After the ideas have been generated, sifted, and sorted into topics, GLs assign an initial value to them, and both the GLs and the CTMs evaluate the risk associated with the ideas.

At this early stage of the process, GLs often tend to shy away from ideas that are controversial or that they don't support; they also tend to ignore ideas that may be promising but are embryonic.

It is the job of the CTMs to help the GLs work through their discomfort and look at everything. This process is the organization's opportunity to look at and make smart decisions about controversial ideas. While ultimately no GL will be asked to implement an idea that he or she does not believe in, rejecting one at this stage is not acceptable. GLs also need to understand that it's okay to have some high-risk ideas that really stretch thinking but with which they are not comfortable, and also some "placeholder" ideas that are not very well developed and need more fleshing out.

Steering Committee Review 1

The end of Step 1 is marked by SCR 1, the first Steering Committee Review. At this meeting, the CTMs assist each GL to present their initial ideas for review. The SCMs will have been primed by the CTMs about the GLs' progress and about any missing ideas. The SCMs are also using the first review to test the GLs' commitment. They need to ensure that all GLs are fully engaged, and during SCR 1, they will get a sense of which Groups may need encouragement or help. Are the controversial ideas included in the portfolio? Has the GL really stretched his or her thinking? Are there ideas in the portfolio that the GL is absolutely against? The GLs' success will be judged not just by the way they present but also by content and knowledge. They are also expected to advocate ideas they favor. In judging a GL's performance, SCMs consider these questions:

- Have all areas been addressed?
- Do the ideas describe actions that can be taken?
- Does the GL have a strong understanding of how the ideas will affect the Group's baseline?
- Is the GL's understanding of the ideas strong enough to stand up to SCM scrutiny?

At this point, ideas will still be in the early stages of development. Ideas from any one Group may conflict with ideas from another. Some ideas will seem dumb. All of this is okay and is normal for this stage of the process.

Because SCMs will hear from all of the Groups in the organization, they will also get a sense of just how big the opportunity is. This first review is one in which SCMs should listen, not comment. Good ideas may be killed prematurely if SCMs indicate too early in the process which ones they dislike. At this stage, SCMs also have to be careful not to discourage people or shoot down ideas, because GLs may have taken a risk in putting controversial ideas forward. SCMs also should not praise Groups that are clearly struggling, as doing so will quash any hope of that Group ever generating good ideas.

> A core project goal for SCR 1 is to make sure all the ideas have been surfaced. The goal is for a complete portfolio. At this stage, it doesn't matter if some ideas within a Group conflict with others.

Some general questions for SCMs to consider across the company at this point include the following:

- What ideas are missing?
- What key themes are emerging across the Groups? (These are called Cross-Group Topics.)

- Are there ideas that are so obvious and simple they can be implemented right away?

After the first SCR, GLs need to identify the analysis that will be needed to support ideas going forward. CTMs should start to think about the ideas with medium or high ratings and how they can work to build consensus by challenging the issues with analysis or modifying ideas to mitigate valid concerns. The final responsibility of the SCMs is to set high aspirations for change for Steering Committee Review 2 (SCR 2).

> A Group's idea list should be organized by topic. It should reflect ideas from all of the processes people spend their time on and where, according to the baseline, money is spent.

G. VALUING, RISK RATING, AND DEBATING (STEP 2)

The goal of Step 2 of the process is to do the following:

- Accurately value all the ideas in the portfolio
- Coordinate ideas across Groups
- Learn about the risks of the ideas from those potentially affected by them
- Debate how to overcome the risks

Valuing an idea means figuring out how much money the company would earn if it is implemented. Each idea in the portfolio is given a value by the GL, who will face challenges in valuing some of the ideas. How much time can be saved by doing something in a streamlined way? Where time is saved, GLs need to estimate the time savings and then convert them into real savings that the company can capture. GLs also have to make sure that they are not double-counting savings. If there are two ideas to save the same expenses, only one of them (the lowest-risk idea) will count toward the savings.

GLs are always encouraged to value an idea conservatively. In this way, when the idea eventually outperforms and has more impact than agreed, the GLs are seen as winners. Aim low, shoot high!

If an idea includes some sort of automation or technology cost in order to make it happen, the chances are that GLs will not know how to figure out these implementation costs. As we have seen, the process includes a separate information technology (IT) process to review these ideas and to estimate automation costs.

You might think that technology costs would be a huge part of any change project as people figure out ways to replace their manual processes with systems and automation. Clients are always surprised by the relatively small number of ideas that involve technology spending. Across the projects I have been involved with, on average, fewer than 10 percent of the projects' ideas required tech spending to implement. Most ideas do *not* involve changes in technology. This is due in part to the tight rules for an idea to count—it must be implemented in 36 months, and it must pay for itself within 4 years. But those are not the major reasons. Many more ideas involve simply changing the way things are done without involving technology.

During our process, we record all ideas and their values on a computer system called Phoenix. This system allows GLs to know at any time the total amount of savings their ideas are suggesting. The system also records risk ratings and whether an idea is collectively Low, Medium, or High Risk. It also produces easy-to-read reports for Steering Committee Meetings. This saves much time in the meetings as every Group has the same report, in the same format, with the numbers calculated in exactly the same way. It allows the SCMs to compare one Group with another.

Many large ideas have an impact across more than one Group, and these ideas are coordinated by Cross-Group Topic teams. These teams are led by CTMs, and they have representation from more than one Group. I typically find that 10 to 25 major ideas in a project—often those that are the largest and most complex—require this kind of treatment. The team itself figures out the ideal solution for a Cross-Group Topic, not an individual GL. For example, in a bank, one such topic might be the same one we introduced in chapter 9—the idea to streamline the credit review process. Doing this will involve input from the people who make loans (the lenders), the people who approve them (the credit department), and the people who review the loans (the loan review department). Any idea to streamline the process will result in savings to each of those departments, and they all need to be on board with the changes.

In Step 2, all people affected by an idea participate in risk rating it, based on how risky they perceive it to be—Low, Medium, or High. Anytime an idea is rated Medium or High, the risk rater must say why that rating is assigned. This explanation allows the debate to begin. During Step 2, the GLs and CTMs begin to understand who is opposed to each idea and why. This is the first stage in beginning to build consensus.

Steering Committee Review 2

This step also finishes with a review—SCR 2. By the end of this step, there will be coordination across the Groups, the savings will be calculated accurately, and much of the risk rating will have been completed. Toward the end of Step 2, the main task changes to building consensus, the entire focus of the next step.

In SCR 2, the SC's role is much different from its role in SCR 1. Now is the time for SCMs to fully understand the ideas and to begin to debate them. Each GL meets with the SC for about 30 minutes as the GL presents his or her major ideas for change. Themes begin to emerge across Groups. The goal for the SC is to encourage GLs to be as aggressive as they can in thinking about ways to change their business without introducing unnecessary risk into the organization.

H. BUILDING CONSENSUS (STEP 3)

If there is a secret to our simple change process, the PGI Promise®, it is building consensus, Principle 8.

At the end of the process, the goal for GLs is to have presented a portfolio of ideas that delivers the greatest impact and overlooks no significant opportunities. Building consensus plays a key part in developing such portfolios. It guarantees that any idea that is committed to is doable and that everyone who will be affected by it has had a say in its genesis.

While Principle 8 is the secret for ensuring 100 percent implementation, success depends on all of the other principles as important ingredients: principles such as the importance of picking the right people for the Catalyst Team; ownership of ideas; making it hard to take ideas out of the system; consideration of ideas must be based on facts and analysis; and nothing less than 100 percent implementation is acceptable.

In our process, consensus isn't about selecting the lowest common denominator of an idea—the place where everyone accepts there is no risk. It isn't about everyone being in perfect agreement and harmony. It is about reducing the risk associated with an idea to a level that all affected parties are comfortable with while not compromising the idea's value. In our parlance, it does not mean that there is no risk; it means that the benefits outweigh the risks. By Step 3, the number of ideas still in play will have been dramatically reduced: duplicates will have been removed, similar ideas will have been consolidated, and truly high-risk ideas will have been put onto the back burner.

The ones that remain have received detailed valuation and wider risk rating. Before SCR 1, only the CTMs and the GLs risk rated the ideas. By SCR 3, anyone else affected by each idea has had the chance to risk rate it and debate it.

The goal of Step 3 is to build consensus, and a key aspect of that is "upgrading" ideas—moving as many ideas to the low-risk category as possible. Upgrading can be about splitting ideas and figuring out what its low-risk and high-risk components are. It can be about changing the idea to accommodate a specific concern. And it can be about reducing the scope of an idea if it is overextending. Without the goal of reaching consensus, big ideas can be killed because someone objects to just one component. Another principle also protects ideas: analysis must be based on fact, not opinion.

The main part of the CTMs' job at this stage is to find creative ways to think about ideas and ferret out opportunities for compromise and brokered solutions. Out of all their responsibilities, the CTMs' role in building consensus is the most vital. Here ideas will either live or die. It stands to reason that many of the ideas that initially lack consensus are controversial, high-profile, big-money ones.

Think back once more to the case where the bank's head of operations wanted to reduce the call center hours. He rated the idea as low risk. The head of retail, who wanted the center kept open 24/7, rated the idea high risk. The CTMs asked the head of retail to explain his reasons, and he did so, supporting his stance with facts, including that every one of the bank's competitors had a 24/7 call center.

The CTMs had to see if there was any room for compromise or if there were any other facts that were not being considered. They persuaded the head of retail to sit in the call center in the middle of the night, where he was able to see the low value of the calls that came in. He then changed his mind about the importance of a 24/7 call center.

Sometimes consensus is built not by changing someone's mind but by modifying an idea. I worked with an insurance company that required eight signatures on any new policy over $1 million. An idea was submitted to change the threshold from $1 million to $5 million. Another suggestion was to lower the number of required signatures from eight to two. A compromise was reached that for any policy of $2.5 million or below, two signatures would suffice. For any policy higher than that, four would be needed.

When consensus cannot be reached, an idea will not go forward. Good ideas don't get abandoned very often, thanks to clever CTMs, but it does happen. In my experience, I have found it is better to abandon an idea than to commit to one without consensus, because objectors will find a way to kill it eventually, and a lot of time and money will have been wasted.

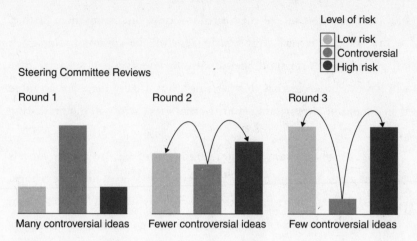

EXHIBIT 11.5   Building Consensus

As Exhibit 11.5 shows, by the time SCR 3 comes along, consensus has been built on most ideas, and few remain controversial.

Office Hours

Immediately before SCR 3, it is important to ensure that all the senior executives, the SCMs, fully understand the ideas for change that the GLs are recommending. My team and I do this through what are called Office Hours. The SCMs don't spend much time on the change process other than at the three reviews, but each spends a day with CTMs and GLs toward the end of the process, without other SCMs present, where they can fully understand the ideas, ask their own questions, and have any lingering concerns addressed. After Office Hours, they are completely prepared for SCR 3.

Steering Committee Review 3

As with the other steps, Step 3 finishes with an SCR. Here the goal is very different: it is to make decisions.

All the issues about ideas have been raised, all the debate has taken place, consensus has been built, and few issues remain. The SC has debated the major and controversial ideas at least twice and probably has spent hours outside of the formal meetings discussing them further. At this stage, it is very clear which ideas will be approved and which will be rejected. A small number of ideas may remain controversial (they will have to be decided at this meeting), but usually there are no more than a handful of remaining controversial ideas across all the presenting Groups.

SCR 3s go very fast. It is not unknown for GLs to appear for less than a minute. A GL might say, "Here is my portfolio of ideas for change. Of my 100 ideas, 58 are low risk, and everybody who has looked at them believes they are low risk. I recommend these as 'go' ideas. Everyone agrees that the other 42 ideas are all either medium- or high-risk ones. These should be 'no go' ideas. I have no controversial ideas in my portfolio." In this case, the CEO may then ask, "Are you sure you are committing to all these ideas? You know I expect you to deliver on them." Upon receiving confirmation, the SC would approve all the ideas (and the actions and savings associated with them) en masse.

In one sense, the dynamics of SCR 3 take decision making out of the hands of the senior executives on the SC. It is very difficult for any senior executive *not* to agree with GLs who come forward with a complete set of well-thought-out ideas about which everyone in the organization agrees.

I. IMPLEMENTATION PLANNING

As soon as a GL leaves SCR 3, implementation planning begins for that Group. The first step is to gather the approved ideas into "projects," each one dealing with similar ideas. Each project is then assigned a Project Manager, who will be responsible for implementation of the ideas in his or her project.

The GL then assigns timing to the ideas. Implementation can occur over 36 months; the GL is asked to assign a preferred completion time to each idea. This preferred timing is just a starting point for many of the ideas. The GL will have constraints on implementing ideas where coordination is needed:

- If the idea affects another Group, that Group will need to be involved in timing.
- If the idea is dependent on technology spending, the technology department will need to review the timing in light of other demands on it.
- If the idea has personnel considerations, the HR department will need to produce a forward-looking plan.

While the GL is forming the Group implementation plan, other areas are also busy planning. The technology department will prioritize its work based on which ideas produce the biggest impact and are easiest to do. It also needs to combine new ideas with its existing development ideas into a new "slate." The IT department may staff up temporarily to take care of the new but short-term demand.

The HR department is also building a company-wide plan for the future. Where have jobs gone away and where have they been created (either in the revenue ideas or in ideas to insource certain functions)? How can these needs be matched? The finance department is busy building the new cost savings and revenues into the budgets so that they can be measured. And the communications team prepares a package to explain to employees the results of the project and some of the great ideas that have been approved.

J. ENSURING 100 PERCENT IMPLEMENTATION

We know from the principles how important it is to achieve 100 percent implementation. I have never worked on a project where less than 100 percent has been achieved. This is quite a claim. But here I am claiming the success of others. The reason for this success is that the companies I have worked with have set 100 percent implementation as a goal and have not veered from it. And they have put in the structure to ensure that all approved ideas are fully implemented. In our process, 100 percent implementation is assured because of the following actions:

Visible Commitment to Ideas

The GLs have risk rated as Low the approved ideas and have stated in a public forum, in front of the SCMs, that they want to implement those ideas. The GLs own the ideas and want to do them; for this reason, there is little backtracking once an idea has been approved.

Consensus Built around Ideas

Everyone impacted by the ideas has had the chance to have his or her say. Their concerns have been overcome, and they have risk-rated the ideas Low. They are unlikely to undermine ideas they have agreed to after compromise.

Senior Management Approved Ideas

Senior managers have listened to the ideas and had the chance to debate them. They have approved the ideas in a public setting.

Risks and Implementation Costs Calculated in Advance

During the process, the GLs carefully valued all approved ideas and then agreed to capture the impact of each one. All the implementation costs associated with the ideas have been calculated and approved in advance. There are no surprises.

Implementation Coordinators Monitor Progress

A small number of CTMs stay behind full time and do not return to their regular jobs for up to a year in order to track results. They are not responsible for implementing the ideas, but if an idea goes off track, they will know about it early and help the GL get it back on track again. They continue to report to the SC on a monthly basis. If an idea is failing, GLs are expected to attend the SC meeting to report on what they intend to do about it.

Tracking Systems Report Results

Implementation is tracked in three ways to ensure that the implementation steps happened and the idea was implemented, that any HR consequences took place, and that the financial savings resulting from the idea showed up. The tracking system includes an early-warning system so that the SC can quickly learn of any ideas that go off track. There are always a small number of ideas that don't go as expected. But these are more than made up for by others that outperform the conservative expectations. GLs have committed not just to the ideas but also to producing a financial result. In the very rare case that an idea goes off track, GLs have a whole bank of other ideas they can turn to in order to make up missing financial results.

All of these activities ensure that the ideas are implemented and that 100 percent of the value of the ideas is captured.

K. THE ROLE OF THE PROJECT PARTNERS

Undergoing change is very difficult for any organization, and there will be many challenges along the way. One final key ingredient to the success of a change project is the group of external "Project Partners," or consultants, the company chooses to work with. An "experienced" team will likely have little knowledge of the company that engages them and may well not know the industry either. But this doesn't matter. They need a different kind of experience. The key skill Project Partners need to demonstrate is a keen understanding of human behavior. The Project Partners' goal is to help generate 10,000 debates about ideas for change and then to help quickly resolve them by building consensus. To do this, they need to be smart, fearless, empathetic, and respectful, but it is also their obligation to firmly challenge any of the project participants when appropriate. Working with and understanding managers is critical to success.

SUMMARY

During the one hundred days of the project, there is a lot of enthusiasm and energy throughout the entire organization, which is part of the rationale for involving everyone. As implementation begins and people see change happening—not merely being talked about—they begin to expect not only rapid change but continuous change going forward. People expect their ideas to be listened to in the future, not ignored. The process has changed the culture of the organization, but it will not be sustainable without extra measures to maintain and reinforce that culture change. People must learn to be vigilant about keeping the barriers broken; shooting down barriers must become intrinsic to the way people operate.

The end of our process signals a new beginning for the company.

CHAPTER 12

MINING GOLD: THE RESULTS TO EXPECT

"**K**NOWING WHAT I KNOW NOW, NEIL, I WOULD HAVE done this project even if there was no significant financial gain," the chief executive of an East Coast company told me after his project was finished. This surprised me, as he had just approved ideas worth $200 million a year to his bottom-line profit as the result of the project. His was an excellent company to work with. The employees were enthusiastic, and there was genuine camaraderie and humor across his management team—something you do not see in every organization. His senior colleagues really enjoyed each other's company.

"Why is that, Rick?" I asked, slightly bemused.

"It is about simplicity," he replied. "We've approved more than 2,000 ideas, and most of them are about making us simpler—simpler to do business with for our customers and simpler for our associates to work with each other. You can already see what an effect that is having on the morale of our people."

Rick was right. Making the way you do things simpler is one of the key results coming out of a barrier-busting project. The results fall into three categories:

1. Reducing complexity
2. Financial impact
3. Culture change

The amount of change in each category is hugely significant.

REDUCING COMPLEXITY

In every company I have worked with, a huge number of change ideas are approved. Most result in reducing complexity within the organization and in making life simpler for employees. When you reduce the number of chocolate flavors from more than 30 to 8 at a food manufacturer, you reduce the amount of paperwork and the number of checks the finance department has to write, and you make an inventory count a lot easier. In fact, most of the ideas generated in a change process result in an easier way of doing business.

The resulting simplicity was not the only thing about the process that impressed Rick. He was stunned by the number of ideas that were surfaced. He had about 10,000 people in his organization, and they generated around 8,000 ideas for change. "I just wouldn't have believed that in a successful company such as ours there were more than 2,000 ways we could reduce costs or improve revenues," he said.

Neither the results Rick's company achieved nor his response was unusual. Let me share some statistics. As a rule of thumb, I expect to see on average one raw idea surfaced per employee; I have worked with a company that had just over 2,000 employees, as well as one with slightly fewer than 300,000—and many sizes in between. Over the years, I have witnessed literally hundreds of thousands of ideas surfacing. The minimum has been 2,000 at one of my smallest clients to 150,000 ideas during the first half of a project at a large global company.

Of course, these are the raw ideas. The number of approved ideas is fewer; it ranges from 600 to 4,000. This range is surprisingly narrow, given that I work with companies of all sizes. Companies, no matter their size, seem to approve roughly the same number of ideas (2,000 on average); what changes is the size of an idea's impact. The larger the company, the greater the impact of an individual idea.

The type of ideas that are approved also range from the very large strategic business ideas (remember the chief operating officer's pet middle-market business we discussed in chapter 1) to small ideas that change the way a process works. Big, controversial ideas get raised in a safe environment. But smaller ideas are equally important, and you cannot lose sight of them. While their financial impact might be low, they contribute hugely to reducing complexity. As we have already discussed, one of the reasons that ideas are sought from the entire organization is because ideas that people have been itching to raise, the ones that will make their lives easier and their customers' lives easier, also get surfaced. They may be small by dollar amount—if their value is even measurable—but the ideas are not small to the people who suggest them, particularly if they are going to change the way employees do their everyday jobs.

One client surfaced 1,200 ideas just for improving the way its call centers were managed. The ideas were simple enough that the company implemented them at a rate of sixty a week. They included such minor changes as giving customer service representatives a drop-down menu to get to the screen relevant to the client's issue instead of having to scroll to the appropriate screen.

An insurance company changed from a "push" to a "pull" system in its claims resolution department. In a push system, each rep is allocated a certain number of claims a day. In a push system, claims are sent to reps regardless of whether they are ready to take on new ones. Some reps finished early as soon as their daily quota was hit. But when the reps were dealing with complicated claims, they were not always able to get to all of the ones in their queue, so there would be unresolved claims at the end of a shift. There was no way for claims to get "pushed" back into the system, so these claims went to a special "overflow" handling area, and their resolution was delayed.

When the department switched to a pull system, reps could "grab" a claim when they were free, with the result that claims got resolved more quickly. This cost nothing to implement and had the added benefit of giving people a sense of control over their own work. Department morale improved measurably. The company still managed how much work people did, but it took a different approach to managing it—measuring the number of claims a month each rep completed. This idea saved some money because some employees now handled more claims rather than finishing early, but the financial impact was not significant. However, this less complex process was much better for both employees and customers, and it eliminated the need for an overflow department.

When the goal is to reduce complexity, even the smaller value ideas count.

One of the best results of a good change process is what I call "the creative ideas." These are the truly unexpected ones that surface when people are free to suggest anything, knowing that their ideas will at least be considered. These ideas are often surprising in their simplicity and cleverness. We have already seen some examples: pooling blood for HIV testing, adding right turns to delivery routes to make them longer but more efficient, and getting both parties in a credit card dispute on the phone.

Some actions companies take can be downright ingenious. Can you imagine the looks on people's faces when a product development person came up with the idea to put the label on a ketchup bottle upside down? They must have thought he had been working too hard or too late when he suggested that idea. But it actually makes a lot of sense. Ketchup is a colloid, and people always need to turn the bottle upside down and shake it to get the ketchup to flow. And an upside-down bottle takes up less valuable refrigerator space. This no-cost solution (not actually the result of my work or the process) boosted the company's market share, which is the key to success in the food services business.

Some of the ideas for change that will come up will resolve what appear to be dumb things a company is doing—and every company has a few of those. (Remember the credit card company that was sending its customers a card valid for just a month and the company that was mailing customer statements to itself as part of its "green" initiative?) One consumer goods company was spending more than $100,000 a year honoring competitors' coupons. The smart solution to this dumb practice was to stop doing it. The company had employed someone whose job it was to monitor coupons, but during a cost-cutting exercise, the company had decided that her $40,000-a-year salary wasn't worth it. No one had figured out how much money she was actually saving the company or how to make sure that her work still got done.

Every company has some interesting statistics that leave you shaking your head—and can point to opportunity for change. At least two companies I have worked with had more active laptops than they had people—1.4 laptops per person was the worst ratio I have seen. Yet another company had more BlackBerrys than it had people. And one large bank had four times more internal passwords than it had employees. Why does this matter? Because the passwords were tracked on a database and frequently changed—all of which required monitoring and work.

Ideas come in different sizes, and they also come in different types. They will come flooding in as soon as employees believe you genuinely want to receive them. Almost every idea will help reduce complexity—one of the major results of a change project.

FINANCIAL IMPACT

By far the most staggering result of a good change process is the financial impact. It is one of the measures of success and one that cannot be argued with. I calculate financial impact by taking the total of the results and measuring it as a percentage of the previous year's profits. On average, this number is 25 percent—profits have increased by an average of 25 percent. For most companies this is a huge number. Across the projects I have worked on, the results have ranged from an increase in pretax profits of $37 million a year at one of the smallest companies to more than $5 billion a year at the largest. The percentage is independent of the size of the company or the industry; a company that manages real estate investment trusts achieves exactly the same results as an employment agency. In Exhibit 12.1, you can see illustrative results for individual companies across a number of industries.

> Regardless of the size of a company or the industry it is in, the impact of change is the same: an average increase in profits of 25 percent or more should be expected.

Percent of previous year's earnings

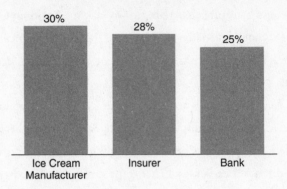

EXHIBIT 12.1 Illustrative Financial Results Across Industries

The total impact is calculated by adding the individual results associated with each idea. Each of the approved ideas is assigned a dollar amount that will affect the bottom line and will be realized once the idea is fully implemented. The Group Leader adds up the total impact of all the ideas he or she has committed to; that is the target number to which he or she will be held. Some of the ideas may not be completed for three years (36 months), so the full impact will not be seen until then. However, most of the financial impact comes quickly; as mentioned, about 60 to 70 percent of the ideas are implemented in the first year.

Not all of the impact needs to be taken to the bottom line—the company can choose how much it saves and how much it spends. The large size of the results allows companies to reinvest some money for growth, as well as to improve short-term profits.

CULTURE CHANGE

The culture change that a project brings about is just as important as the financial change. Culture change is critical to breaking the three behavioral barriers: Barrier 1, Avoiding Controversy; Barrier 3, Reluctance to Change; and Barrier 5, Management Blockers. And it is important to fixing elements of two others: Barrier 2, Poor Use of Time, and Barrier 8, Existing Processes. It is also the key to ensuring that the barriers stay down and that new ideas are surfaced rather than hidden going forward.

As a change process forces barriers to be broken down and as managers behave differently, culture change begins to kick in. Avoiding Controversy is no longer acceptable. Managers who have shown Reluctance to Change are rewarded for taking risks. Management Blockers are exposed and discouraged.

The behavioral change needs to start at the top, and senior management needs to lead by example. Good behaviors need to be spotlighted and rewarded; bad practices need to be highlighted and punished.

As we discussed earlier, as a change process progresses, I typically see examples of culture change beginning to take hold. The new culture manifests itself in new ways of doing things. Are people suddenly more receptive to ideas, including revisiting ideas that got buried? Are you seeing collaboration from a surprising source? Do managers still rely on committees to decide things, or do they now make instant decisions? Do employees go to as many meetings, and do they still travel to internal meetings? When a senior executive tells her finance area that the regular twenty-page report needs to be reduced to ten pages or fewer, culture change is taking hold. As people become conscious of cost and complexity and know that there is an organizational focus on reducing them, they manage their own actions a lot more closely than they used to.

> Culture change ensures that barriers remain broken going forward…and makes sure that ideas do not remain hidden in the future.

Organizations need to make sure that they don't revert to their old way of doing things. If companies don't take extra steps to preserve the culture change, the danger is that there will be no ongoing pressure on managers to continue to change their behavior. In that case, behavior will revert to previous patterns, barriers will reappear, and good ideas will be left unimplemented once more.

After their project, most companies I have worked with adopt a process for continuous improvement that is almost a miniature version of their change process. This is done not just to seek additional new ideas but in order to preserve the culture change. In the early days, there are not a lot of new ideas because the organization has already implemented them all. But an ongoing, continuous improvement process provides a mechanism in the company for the barriers to be beaten down if they arise again. You will recall that we discussed other ways a company can preserve culture change in chapter 9. Below Dr. Richard Levak also discusses how to change culture when he addresses reward systems and punishments.

One of the ways I know that culture change actually occurs in the companies I work with is that I don't get invited back. In my early consulting life, we always tried to sell a client the next project when we were three-quarters of the way through the current one. But a good change process is something you need to do only once. I have yet to find a previous client for whom the bad habits have returned.

HOW TO CHANGE CORPORATE CULTURE

By *Dr. Richard Levak*

> We are what we repeatedly do. Excellence, then, is not an act but a habit.
>
> —Aristotle

> Habit is habit and not to be flung out of the window by any man but coaxed downstairs a step at a time.
>
> —Mark Twain

As most people know, breaking habits is difficult. We develop them for good reason. They allow us to function for periods of time without awareness, saving consciousness for more demanding tasks. In this way, habitual behavior can benefit companies, because it leaves people with the mental bandwidth for important things.

Yet habit is the enemy of change, precisely because it means our actions have become unconscious, their rationale lost over time. To change people's habits and shape new behavior, we first need to understand how people learn and what motivates them.

People adopt behaviors because of reward and punishment—doing things that are rewarding and abandoning things that are punishing. Burned once, you avoid the same situation. Feel rewarded, and you go back for more. The more immediate the reward or the punishment, the more quickly you learn to adopt or avoid behavior. If every time you press a lever you get $20, you will quickly learn to keep on pressing.

Once you have become accustomed to a reward and it suddenly stops, you will press the lever a few times but eventually realize that there is no more reward and stop trying. You might occasionally return and press the lever to see if the largesse has returned, but after a few presses, you will conclude that it is no longer working and stop.

A behavior learned with intermittent rewards, however, can continue long after the rewards have ceased. That's why people keep gambling in the face of loss; having won sometimes, they are seeking the next win, never knowing when it will come.

In a corporation, reward and punishment are often not immediate. They are given out overtly through reviews and feedback and subtly through gestures and indirect actions. The messaging can be further complicated by competing subcultures that reward and punish different behaviors.

The subtle and sporadic nature of rewards and punishments in the corporate world can act as a drag on change because people continue to seek rewards for previously approved behavior. The benefits of a new value system are not always apparent. If they are not compelling, people will not be motivated to fight old habits and create new ones. Just as parental inconsistency is manifested in children's inconsistent behavior, corporate values need to be clear and consistent and people need to be rewarded for adherence. When values and the behaviors that manifest them have been outmoded, new values have to be clearly articulated, and rewards must be instituted to ensure speedy acceptance.

REWARD VERSUS PUNISHMENT

Research shows that rewarding good behavior is more effective in promoting desired behavior than punishing bad behavior. Punishment can make people angry, resentful, and vindictive. Also, when the threat of punishment diminishes, the undesirable behaviors resurface. Keeping negative feedback to a minimum and acknowledging when people do the right thing has been shown to be more effective in promoting and maintaining change.

People also learn from watching others. According to research, the quickest way to change someone's behavior is to put him or her with a group of peers who exhibit the desired behavior. Finally, people can be manipulated into doing things based on the cues given by someone else in the group.

CHANGING BEHAVIOR

Corporate culture is an interlocking series of expectations, rituals, and habits maintained by peer influence and rewarding adherence. To change the way people do things, first you must convince them of the value of change. This is done most effectively by showing them the potential rewards for the new behavior. However, since the rewards are often in the future while the pain of change is immediate, the rewards have to be clearly articulated to serve as motivation.

Given the importance of peer influence, people need to perceive that respected peers are adopting change. According to research, 3 percent of the population tends to be innovators of change, 9 percent are early adopters, 38 percent are early-majority adopters, 38 percent are later-majority adopters, and 12 percent are laggards. Consequently, culture change should be aimed at the early and later majorities because they are the largest groups and will influence the others.

Management cannot espouse change while continuing to operate according to the old paradigm. Employees will do as management does rather than as it says. While performance reviews and training can articulate corporate expectations and financial rewards serve to reinforce them, it is the actions of senior leadership that ultimately create and define corporate culture.

CHAPTER 13

CONCLUSION: WHAT ARE YOU WAITING FOR?

BY NOW YOU KNOW THE HIDDEN BARRIERS THAT cause even excellent companies to do dumb things and that prevent great ideas from surfacing.

You understand the principles for change, you know why psychology is a critical element for success, you know how the change process works, and you know the kind of dramatic results a good change process can bring to a company.

I hope that you also now have a sense of how the eight barriers are showing up in your own company and, in particular, what behavioral barriers are holding you back. You probably have already thought of some good ideas for change. Most important, you may now suspect that the employees in your company have hundreds if not thousands of ideas for change.

I began this book with the supposition that your company is an excellent one. But I also believe that even in such companies there is significant opportunity for improvement. In fact, the opportunity exists in every company, no matter its size, its industry, its level of success and whether it has previously undertaken major improvement initiatives. I have yet to find a company in which the employees do not have significant ideas for change. And you know you can test this very easily just by asking them. If you know the barriers exist, so do the opportunities.

Many years ago, when I realized this perpetual "pot of gold" existed, I was excited and passionate about it. I couldn't understand why all companies wouldn't immediately stop what they were doing and turn to barrier busting. After all, who wouldn't want a 25 percent profit increase? Think of all the extra investment that could be done with those profits.

And there was another benefit. Unlike many "blue sky" strategy projects, the results of a change project could be easily measured. As compensation is based on the results of a project, how could a company lose?

The first problem was one of credibility. I started doing these projects in earnest with small banks in the early 1990s, when financial institutions were facing severe challenges. As the word about early project successes began to spread, the answer came back: "Ah, but we're different. What will work for small banks wouldn't work for a bank of our size." Then, in 1999, because a chief executive officer took a chance on me and the company I worked with, I had the good fortune to lead a project at a very successful large regional bank with 25,000 people; it was the first time such a project had been done at an institution of this size. The project was so successful that it was highlighted on the front cover of the bank's annual report.

"It's okay in a regional bank, but this will never work for an industry leader as we do things very differently and we are already very good" was the next response. But in the early 2000s, the CEO at the top financial institution in the United States (at least according to *Forbes* and the *American Banker*) was very forward-thinking. His bank was large (30,000 people in 83 countries) and very successful. The project I led produced annual profit improvement of $309 million a year—pretty good results at an industry-leading company. But even this was insufficient for project naysayers. I was told that what would work in banking would not work in other industries—until I showed that it could work by leading a first venture into another industry: the logistics and moving industry.

When you have completed enough successful projects across many industries and many geographies, across many companies of varying sizes, and have brought about change at both strong and weak performers, you no longer face the problem of lack of credibility. Senior executives accept that opportunity exists within their company. After all, if it exists everywhere else, why would their organization be the exception? So they must have other reasons for not doing a project.

All managers try to leave a legacy in their department before they move on to greater things. Were they well liked or respected? What changes did they make? How did the department run under them? A CEO is no different—all CEOs try to leave their mark on the company. And CEOs can leave their mark in many ways: they can shake up the management, make an acquisition, enter a new market, or undertake a change project like the one described in this book.

The problem is that company CEOs (and department managers) can undertake perhaps only three major initiatives a year out of many to choose from. A major change project competes for an executive's time with many other initiatives. The challenge for the chief executive is determining when the time is right to do a change project . . . and the right time does come for every company. Sometimes it can be spurred by an internal event (such as a new CEO who wants to make an early mark), or it can be spurred by the prospect of an economic downturn. Companies can always find excuses for not undertaking change, but sooner or later, every company has to figure out ways to reduce complexity and improve the bottom line.

Success in a change project is measured not only by a reduction in complexity (and the better customer service that goes with it) but also by the impact on profits. That component is easy to figure out. From a sheer financial perspective, delay is very costly. One measure we use is "the cost of a day's delay." If your company could gain the average 25 percent increase in profitability that comes from a change project, every two weeks that you delay is costing your company one of those percentage points. For Rick and his East Coast company, it was almost $1 million every working day. For the large global company with $5 billion in opportunity, the cost of a delay was $20 million per day!

But delay is costing you in other ways as well. You are losing the opportunity to engage your workforce in an exciting initiative to improve both the employee and the customer experience. Employees become more engaged and enthusiastic about their work. An employee at one company I worked with looked at this in an extreme way, but what she said had the ring of truth: "It's like going to work for a new company without having to go looking for a new job!" Reducing complexity also improves the customer experience. Insurance claims are processed faster, loans are made more quickly, and companies become easier to deal with.

I always try to argue that the real question a company should answer is not why it should undertake a change project but why it *wouldn't* do it.

Think for a minute about your own experiences with companies that you interact with on a daily basis. You no doubt have thought about the occasional dumb things they do and have thought of solutions that seem blindingly obvious. How much more would you enjoy your interactions with the company if it implemented some of your ideas for change?

The reason for the success of a good change process is not a company's sudden discovery and understanding of the barriers or the ability to get companies to recognize them. The success does not come from how well the company adopts the principles for change or our methodology. It does not come because ideas for change surface. The success is due to buy-in. The strength of a good change process depends on its ability to empower the people who will be impacted by it. Our process gives people the chance to be heard, lets them know that their ideas count, allows them to shape the solutions, grants them ownership, and keeps them accountable. Just as it is true that the eight barriers plague every company, it is also true that every company has the means within it to break those barriers.

The process described in this book allows employees to be the architects of change. The role of my team and I is to facilitate and navigate. We don't stick around for implementation; we leave that up to our clients. But we leave when we do because both we and the company know with a high degree of certainty that change will happen.

The results of the change process are more invigorated, more efficient employees; happier, more satisfied customers; millions of dollars realized in increased profits or for investment; and a simpler way of doing things. Nirvana? It sounds like it. What do you have to lose? Why *wouldn't* your company undertake a project like this?

APPENDIX

Some of the excellent companies that my current colleagues and I have worked with over the last 20 years include the following:

AIMCO
Allmerica
Bank of America
BlueCross BlueShield of Tennessee
Cinergy
Comerica
Detroit Edison
Energy East
First National of Nebraska
Fleet
Heinz
Hooper Holmes
KeyCorp
MasterCard
Mellon
NYSE Euronext
North American Van Lines
PNC
State Auto
Union Bank of California

INDEX